Beyond Ego Psychology:
Developmental Object Relations Theory

BEYOND
EGO PSYCHOLOGY

Developmental Object Relations Theory

Rubin and Gertrude Blanck

New York   Columbia University Press   *1986*

05715

Library of Congress Cataloging-in-Publication Data

Blanck, Rubin.
  Beyond ego psychology.

  Bibliography: p.
  Includes index.
  1. Object relations (Psychoanalysis)   2. Psycho-
therapy.   3. Developmental psychology.   I. Blanck,
Gertrude.   II. Title.
BF175.5.O24B55   1986   150.19′5   85–21356
ISBN 0–231–06266–4

Columbia University Press
New York   Guildford, Surrey

Printed in the United States of America

This book is Smyth-sewn.

Dedicated to the memory of
Margaret S. Mahler, M.D.,
whose work will live on.

Contents

Introduction

HISTORIANS of psychoanalytic theory construction note that psychoanalytic theory has evolved in several phases which, in retrospect, can be more or less distinctly demarcated. Rapaport, writing in 1959, designated four such phases to that date. The first, beginning with Freud's work in the late nineteenth century and terminating in 1897, contains a first approach to ego psychology by introducing a primitive concept of defense. The second phase, from 1897 to 1923, represents Freud's interest in unconscious fantasy and in the instinctual drives. The third phase is marked by the introduction of the structural theory, which led Freud to revise his theory of anxiety, and culminates with Anna Freud's work on the defensive function of the ego and her description of the several mechanisms of defense. The fourth phase begins with Hartmann's introduction of his classic work *Ego Psychology and the Problem of Adaptation,* first presented as a lecture to the Vienna Psychoanalytic Society in 1937 and published in English in 1958. We (1974, 1979) have written extensively on Hartmann's work because of its seminal influence on the ego psychologists who worked with him contemporaneously and on those who followed after him. Rapaport designates this fourth period, from 1937 to 1959, as the phase of ego psychology proper.

Now, a quarter of a century later, theory construction has proceeded, and so much has been added that it is timely to continue in Rapaport's vein and to update his historical survey. With knowledge of that which came after 1937, it seems that the period from 1923 to 1937 should be designated as *early ego psychology,* and the period from 1937 to 1975 as *late ego psychology,* to emphasize that Hartmann's successors—Spitz, Jacobson, and Mahler—paved a new trail in theory construction by following the direction provided by him. We described this in our earlier work.

In 1975 Mahler and her collaborators published the results of their child observation in *The Psychological Birth of the Human Infant*. It introduced a new organizing principle: "A major organization of intrapsychic and behavioral life develops around issues of separation and individuation" (p. 4). We deemed this so important that we found it necessary to add a second volume on ego psychology in order to encompass this new principle which, we believe, alters ego psychology from an important but narrow aspect of psychoanalytic theory to a total psychoanalytic developmental psychology.

Now, once again, we are forced to some new thoughts brought about by expansion of theory. Object relations has been understood to be a function of the ego but, until now, it has been relegated to relative obscurity by being listed as but one of the many ego functions, along with perception, motility, intentionality, anticipation, defense, adaptation, and many more. It is timely now, because of the explosion in knowledge about human development provided by the later ego psychologists, to give it special emphasis because it is of a different order from some of the other ego functions.

On rereading Freud's writings with the objective of finding the roots of object relations theory, one notices that, as early as 1905, Freud was aware of that facet of human psychology even though his focus, then, was on drive theory. And one finds references to object relations interspersed throughout his subsequent work, in "Mourning and Melancholia" (1917a), to cite but one example. But it was Hartmann's description of the encounter between the neonate and the environment, and his introduction of the concept of mental representation, that heralded the contemporary era in ego psychological object relations theory.

Jacobson extends Hartmann's thoughts about the representational world, while Spitz and Mahler provide conclusions from their independent observations of mother-infant interaction. These studies add a new dimension to object relations theory by describing the development of the human infant. Mahler adds the discovery that psychological birth takes place approximately three years after physical birth in the context of the dyadic relationship.

Because of these discoveries, we are now in a position to present a theory of object relations that is consistent with the mainstream of psychoanalytic thought as it has developed from Freud's work, as it has been expanded by the early ego psychologists, and as it is being joined by the addenda of the later and the contemporary ego psychologists.

There are other developments in contemporary theory construction. Of particular note is the intensified interest in the so-called borderline and narcissistic personalities. We include consideration of these important pathologies in our work. Those who have kept abreast of the current spate of literature on these subjects will note that we omit some theories. This is deliberate. Eclecticism, while appeasing the yearning for integration that exists in all of us by virtue of the synthetic function, must be eschewed. Taking a more disciplined approach, one encounters theories about these pathologies that are inconsistent with ego psychology. Some of these incorporate a few of the contributions of the ego psychologists without crediting them; others flow from basically incompatible assumptions. This does not mean that we are unfriendly to new thought, but we insist upon internal consistency as the essential feature of theory construction. For that reason we omit that which is simply popular or appealing.

We believe also that theory builds upon the most solid foundation where there is considered deliberation about that which preceded it, even though one may decide to revise, to elaborate upon, or even to discard earlier formulations. Although it appears that Freud was an exception, it is generally correct to maintain that theory cannot, like Athene, spring from a single mind. Rather, it accrues like links in a chain. Therefore, we follow the consistent linear evolution of ego psychology from Freud to Anna Freud; to Hartmann, Kris, and Loewenstein; to Jacobson; to Spitz; to Mahler. The works of these theorists are both complementary and sequential.

Neither do we maintain that one must accept all preceding theory merely because it exists. But theory construction that lays claim to being scientific must be not only internally consistent, but also subject to clinical validation. This requires that there be justification for discarding or improving upon theory that has gone before. A case in point is the current reconsideration of Freud's formulations about female sexuality. It exemplifies that theory need be neither retained nor discarded for the trivial reason of exalting or deprecating its innovator. One needs to distinguish between methodologically sound theory construction, on the one hand, and faddism or discipleship, on the other. It is our experience as well as our firm conviction that only disciplined and respectful treatment of that which went before can result in innovation of meaningful new theory that can endure and fulfill its only purpose— to enhance clinical practice.

Inevitably, integration will take place in the long run, but only at "critical periods" in theory construction, to borrow a phrase from Spitz. At present it is too early to know which theories will survive the test of clinical validation, which will be revised, and which discarded. That is the process whereby the several now-incompatible theories will become more cohesive by means of a natural process of selection and survival of the fittest. Then, all that is sound will fit together (in Hartmann's sense). That time has not yet come because we are still in a period of theoretical ferment, particularly around issues that pertain to the borderline and narcissistic conditions.

The growing body of knowledge about very early infant development, and especially about the development of self and object relations, transcends ego psychology as we presented it in 1974 and expands psychoanalytic development psychology beyond our 1979 description of it. The elaborated developmental object relations theory which we present here overlaps earlier theory as well as adds to it.

We shall make a few comments about the technical and diagnostic implications of object relations theory—its effect upon the modes of transference, upon interpretation, upon other interventions. Our principal intent is to convey our expanded thoughts about ego as organization, which we proposed in 1979. As we said then, we do not regard our contributions as finite, but as steps along the way toward an ever-growing body of psychoanalytic theory. Some of it will become integrated in the manner that we have described; some will be improved upon, superseded, or even discarded. We can only know now that theory construction will advance as clinical experience dictates. As Hartmann (1964) has noted, all will seem different in the future.

It will be useful for the reader of our theoretical presentations to bear in mind that metapsychology consists of constructs—abstractions that are used in all sciences as aids to conceptualization. Their only value lies in providing a way to organize concepts and to make sense out of an otherwise bewildering welter of data. They are indispensable to the clinician who is presented with random material that must become organized in his or her mind in order to be interpretable at the appropriate time. Constructs are not subject to the same kinds of proof sometimes possible in the exact sciences. They cannot be weighed, measured, or replicated. One cannot prove the existence of id, ego, superego, or undifferentiated matrix, nor is there need for such proof, since constructs are created to serve organization of theory and may be discarded, revised, or superseded when they are no longer useful.

Beyond Ego Psychology:
Developmental Object Relations Theory

But everything tends to show that . . . we shall be driven by the study of neuroses to assume the existence of many new things which will later on gradually become the subject of more certain knowledge. What is new has always aroused bewilderment and resistance. (Freud 1905a:11)

CHAPTER 1
PSYCHOANALYTIC DEVELOPMENTAL PSYCHOLOGY

EGO PSYCHOLOGY has evolved into so much more than the psychology of the ego that the term itself appears to be a misnomer. Yet historical necessity and common usage are so insistent that we are obliged to retain it. Modifications such as *psychoanalytic developmental psychology* have been suggested. Although that newer term is more descriptive of what ego psychology has become, it has shortcomings as well, the principal one being that it fails to retain connection with its roots in early ego psychology. Now we are proceeding beyond both ego psychology and psychoanalytic developmental psychology, and we seek a new term that will connote that the one has evolved into the other and that both, taken together, become a unified object relations theory. Because there are several object relations theories that must be distinguished one from the other, it is difficult to arrive at a parsimonious term that describes the object relations theory we present here. In order to be accurate as well as descriptive, we offer the term *psychoanalytic developmental object relations theory.* That this is awkward and needs to be replaced by a more abbreviated term is obvious. But we believe that can come about only after the theory is well enough understood to be recognized by a "nickname." For the time being, the more awkward term, while sacrificing elegance for the sake of accuracy, is more appropriate.

In psychoanalytic parlance an object is a person other than the subject. But psychological life does not begin with perception of self and other. Even when perception begins, self and object images are merged. Contemporary ego psychology describes the first three years of life as a dyadic experience during which the merged images separate out gradually into more or less distinct and stable self and object representations.

This suggests that even the term *object relations theory* is somewhat of a misnomer; it should be *self and object relations theory*. This would better reflect the psychology of the early days, weeks, and months of life.

Here we review ego psychology from its origin to the present to trace its historical evolution into a self and object relations theory.

The germ of the concept of *ego* in Freud's thought is to be found in his suggestion in *The Interpretation of Dreams* (1900) that there is a censoring force that prevents unconscious content from entering consciousness. A careful reader of Freud's work can detect that already in 1921 he was arriving at a more sophisticated concept of ego which, by 1923, he was able to define as "a coherent organization of . . . mental processes" (p. 17). His clarity about the ego and its functioning was such by then that he was able, in that same work, to proceed to describe the superego as well as the ego. Thus he provided the tripartite theory of psychic structure that paved the way toward modern ego psychology.

This turning point in psychoanalytic theory construction is one of many. In chronological order there are: the discovery of the repressed and the existence of an unconscious (1895); the discovery of infantile sexuality (1905b); Freud's realization that repressed sexual ideation comes not from real experience but from fantasy (1906). But in terms of its influence upon future theory construction, the discovery that part of the ego is unconscious constitutes the most influential and far-reaching of all of Freud's revisions of theory; it foreshadows all of the developments in ego psychology yet to come. It forced Freud to revise his theory of anxiety three years later (1926). Whereas he had thought earlier of anxiety as the resultant of accumulation of toxins caused by failure to discharge sexual substances, by 1926 he realized that anxiety is the affective consequence of a far more sophisticated process. Repression, he realized, is a mechanism of defense employed by the unconscious part of the ego in response to anxiety as a signal of danger. Its purpose is to relegate material to the unconscious and to maintain it there by exertion of countercathectic energy. This new understanding of the defensive function of the ego was elaborated upon by Anna Freud.

In her later years, Anna Freud rather too modestly downplayed the importance of her contribution, *The Ego and the Mechanisms of Defense* (1936), contending that she meant merely to summarize her father's work as a birthday present to him. The psychoanalytic community views it as vastly more important than a mere festschrift. While there is little doubt that father and daughter had many conversations and that she incorporated his thoughts in her work, her description of the defensive function of the ego and of the defense mechanisms stands in its own right as another milestone in theory construction. Beyond that, she makes a major contribution to the technique of psychoanalysis by demonstrating how the ego functions in the treatment process. No longer is it appropriate for the psychoanalyst to focus on id content alone, but equal attention must be given to the ego—in particular to the operation of the defense mechanisms and of the defensive system as a whole.

Freud established the basic technique of psychoanalysis in 1912–13, and it was codified by Fenichel (1941), Sharpe (1950), Glover (1955), and Menninger (1958). However, little of the implications of ego psychology for technique other than the modifications proposed by Anna Freud have crept into the literature on technique. The early ego psychologists, especially Hartmann (1951), Kris (1951, 1952, 1956a, 1956b, 1956c), and Loewenstein (1951), were profoundly interested in technique and made contributions which are still not fully understood or exploited. For example, in his paper "On Some Vicissitudes of Insight in Psychoanalysis" (1956a), commonly known as the "Good Hour" paper, Kris alludes so subtly to an aspect of technique guided by ego psychological considerations that it is often less than fully appreciated. He describes the "Good Hour" as beginning with a mild negative tinge. Unless one is familiar with each link in the chain of ego psychological theory as it has been added by each of the several ego psychologists, one may miss the fact that this employs the concept of the third organizer of the psyche as described by Spitz (1957). Kris shows that the patient uses the aggressive drive in a developmental thrust. This "negativism" is positive in the sense that, having developed in the course of the treatment, the patient adopts an "I will do it myself" stance analogous to that of the developing child who begins to supplant functions of the object representations by transferring them to the self representations (R. Blanck 1981). We have heard experienced technicians ponder this apparent paradox because they confuse *negative* with *undesirable*. To an ego psychologist it is clear that Kris meant that the so-called negative tinge represents an assertion of autonomy. He contrasts this with the "Pseudo-Good Hour" where excessive hostility is the motivating force for the negativism. The technical consequences of the analyst's failure to make this distinction can lead him or her to regard the positive thrust as undesirable, an error that can be devastating to the progress of an analysis.

Freud (1914b) understood narcissism in a most profound way, and even distinguished the transference neuroses from the narcissistic neuroses in a manner which parallels, surprisingly, our more modern distinction between the structured and the understructured personalities. We, of course, have the benefit of the structural theory, which Freud had not yet arrived at when he wrote about narcissism. Since approximately 1955 or 1960, interest in the understructured personality, usually referred to as narcissistic or borderline, has accelerated because it began to be realized that some such patients are treatable, although techniques that depart from those designed for the neurotic patient had to be devised. Inspired by that interest, more sophisticated theoretical underpinnings for understanding these pathologies have been developed. We have designated these newer theories as *late ego psychology* to distinguish them from the contributions of the pioneeers—Freud, Anna Freud, Hartmann, Kris, and Loewenstein. These late or later ego psychologists have added so much to the understanding of the understructured as well as the structured personalities that it has become the platform upon which much of our work is built.

We find aspects of the newer theory applicable to the structured personality as well as to the understructured, but because psychoanalysts have vastly more experience with structured patients, we have tended to place our emphasis upon the diagnosis and treatment of the more severe pathologies. It is clear, however, that certain ego psychological concepts, such as the relationship between adaptation and defense, play important roles in understanding and interpreting conflict and therefore are of critical importance in the treatment of the structured personalities. We have demonstrated that technical position with the explanation of the "Good Hour" and we shall demonstrate it further as we proceed.

Although the so-called late ego psychologists are contemporaries and overlap one another, each has pursued a separate and unique course in

linking his or her theory to the entirety of the chain of ego ps̱
Much of their work is sequential as well as complementary. ₁
upon Hartmann, who is known as the "father" of ego ps̱
because he provides fundamental concepts which lend themselves to
further theory construction and have important implications for technique as well.

Hartmann

Hartmann defines adaptation as the reciprocal relationship between the
organism and its environment. The neonate, he says, possesses an innate
endowment which varies from one individual to another. This endowment is contained in an undifferentiated matrix. Differentiation in the
physiological sense of specialization of tissue begins in utero, but differentiation in the psychological sense begins only after birth.

The inborn apparatuses or embryonic ego functions are destined to
develop at certain phase-specific times after birth. Normally that development takes place in a conflict-free sphere, even though these functions may later become involved in conflict. Examples of this are
locomotion and speech, among many others. Few children fail to walk
and talk close to the phase-appropriate time, although the unfolding
of those capacities can be delayed by impeded development. But some
of the less observable ego functions such as perception, anticipation,
and reality testing, if delayed or undeveloped, may not be correctable
by belated quickening. Normally, the mothering person, in interaction
with the child, promotes the unfolding of latent functions. This is
object relations theory in its essence.

Adaptation begins at the moment of encounter between the neonate
possessed of adequate endowment in the conflict-free sphere and the
average expectable environment, which is the term Hartmann used to describe the norm on the environmental side of the encounter. *Fitting
together* refers to the regulatory process that maintains equilibrium—
between the individual and the environment; between the instinctual
drives; among the mental institutions; and of the synthetic function
itself.

Adaptation is attained both narrowly and broadly. In the narrow sense, the individual's adaptive mechanism and regulating systems interact with the environment. But they also have an effect upon the environment, requiring new accommodation to an altered environment; thus the process broadens as the scope of adaptive necessity enlarges.

An ego function may attain secondary autonomy where it had been bound in conflict, becoming conflict-free; Hartmann refers to this process as "change in function." He takes into account the fact that conflict may be not only intersystemic, but also intrasystemic—that is, there may be conflict within the ego, between or among the several elements that "reside" there.

The germ of a developmental object relations theory is also to be found in Hartmann's work. He describes an escalation of levels of object relations, from primary narcissism, through need for the object for gratification, to object constancy. Object constancy involves sustained cathexis of the object representation regardless of the state of need. And he takes a major step in the evolution of a theory of narcissism by proposing that it consists, not of cathexis of the ego as Freud thought, but of cathexis of the self (or self representation).

Hartman and His Collaborators

Hartmann, Kris, and Loewenstein extend ego psychology by adding the genetic dimension to the three other features of metapsychology— the dynamic, topographic, and economic. The genetic feature explains why certain solutions to past conflict were adopted. This complements Hartmann's view (personal communication) that, in childhood, all defense is adaptive and only becomes maladaptive later in life because of its rigidity.

They elaborate on the defense mechanism *identification,* showing that it has a developmental in addition to a defensive purpose and that it is clearly a process of internalization. Ego autonomy is attained by means of internalization as the individual becomes less dependent upon the object.

They pay particular attention to the process of superego formation. Preserving Freud's formulation that the superego is the heir to the Oedipus complex, they explain how superego precursors arise in conjunction with ego development by means of introjection, incorporation, and identification, and how these elements combine to form a new structure under the duress of coping with the Oedipus complex.

Hartmann also introduces a new concept of drive taming which he calls *neutralization*. He intends this as an explanation for the transfer of energy from id to ego. After long reflection on this proposition, including attempts to employ it clinically, we find it unnecessary in the light of our rediscovery of Freud's final statement on the drives. In 1979 we reconstructed Freud's 1940 description of libido as a unifying force and aggression as a separating one, and we presented this as his final revision of his drive theory. It renders the problem of drive taming less pressing because it makes it possible to regard the two drives as operating in concert. Therefore, we relegate neutralization to a transitional phase in the history of ego psychological theory construction. When libido was defined more narrowly as a sexual drive and aggression as a destructive drive, the problem of the quantitative distribution of drive energy was vexing because it was feared that, where there is innate overendowment of drive energy, the id could overpower the ego. There is no need for such concern now that the drives are regarded as serving development. Libido powers union at those times when it is developmentally appropriate (in the symbiotic phase, totally; in the process of selective identification, partially), while the aggressive drive powers severance of connections for the purpose of furthering the separation-individuation process. This obviates fears about overendowment of drive energy.

Jacobson

Jacobson used Hartmann's concept of the undifferentiated matrix to propose that, not only ego and id, but also the two drives begin to differentiate from that matrix at birth under the auspices of adequate mothering. Here again we find that developmental theory and object relations theory are indivisible.

The essense of Jacobson's contribution to psychoanalytic theory construction is her emphasis upon differentiation. Therefore, she disputes Freud's views on primary narcissism and primary masochism, arguing

:e there are separate self and object images, there cannot be
whether libidinal (narcissistic) or aggressive (masochistic), of
that does not yet exist. She regards the self as the totality of
:hic and bodily person. Self representations are the representa-
tio.. f the bodily and mental self in the ego.

In a major contribution she describes the establishment of self and
object images out of gratifying and frustrating experiences in the
mother-child dyad. Engrams of experience are retained as images in
memory traces. As the perceptual apparatus matures, the infant begins
to identify sources of experience; thus images of self and of object are
sorted out. At first, magical affective identifications are established, to
be superseded by selective identification—a process whereby traits of
the object images are selected to become internalized aspects of the
self-images. In such manner is identity acquired.

By the end of the first year of life the child possesses a large repertory
of affects by a process that we (1979) have termed *affect differentiation*.
This assumes that affects, too, arise from the undifferentiated matrix,
and that differentiation takes place developmentally. Experiences of gratification provide positive self-images which are essential to growth.
Equally essential are the affects accompanying frustration, ambition,
possessiveness, envy, rivalry, disappointment, and failure, for in their
absence, the child is unable to establish a separate identity.

Sexual identity, Jacobson points out, is an important aspect of identity formation and is based not only on genital difference, but on
observation of the physical and mental behavior of persons of the same
and of the opposite sex.

Object relations theory is contained also in Jacobson's description of
how representations of the self and of the object world are built. Her
formulations apply to normal development as well as to formations where
the self and object worlds are not clearly differentiated.

She pays considerable attention to superego formation. Building upon
Hartmann and Loewenstein (1962), she describes superego formation
in terms of incorporation of ethical values. Regulation of behavior is
accomplished, at first, in interaction with the object world; later it is
replaced by internal regulation. She attributes functions to the superego, some of which are more traditionally regarded as functions of the
ego. Most important is the regulatory function. It regulates not only

behavior and drive discharge, but self-esteem as well. It maintains harmony between moral codes and ego manifestations by controlling discharge processes. It also governs moods and regulates the entire ego state, and it develops and maintains a coherent and consistent defense organization. (See chapter 2.)

Jacobson provides a particularly important revision of Freud's speculations about female superego formation. It might even be said that she is the first to rescue psychoanalytic theory from Freud's errors about female sexuality, lending impetus to the current reformulations of this important matter by later psychoanalytic theorists. While these theorists agree with Freud that the superego as a functional entity is established with the resolution of the Oedipus complex, they propose that that very resolution comes about, not out of fear of castration, but out of affection for the parent of the same sex. Love causes the child to abandon incestuous and parricidal wishes.

But beyond that, Freud was hampered in attempting to account for the acquisition of a strong superego in the girl by his reasoning that oedipal wishes are abandoned in the face of the castration threat. That reasoning left neither opportunity nor incentive for the girl to give up oedipal wishes and to replace them with a strong superego. The logic of that argument led Freud to the conclusion that women do not resolve the oedipal conflict, are content to marry men who resemble their fathers, and are unable to acquire strong superegos. This speculation is still under attack by "feminists" who are, of course, unsophisticated in psychoanalytic theory. They do not know that Freud gave up the notion that masculinity and activity were synonymous, in a 1932 lecture on femininity. In that lecture Freud also reveals the flavor of his reconsideration of the question of female psychology with his women colleagues:

> The ladies, whenever some comparison seemed to turn out unfavorable to their sex, were able to utter a suspicion that we, the male analysts had been unable to overcome certain deeply-rooted prejudices against what was feminine, and that this was being paid for in the partiality of our researches. (1933b:116)

Neither are feminists aware of Jacobson's revisions of Freud's errors about female psychology and the fact that contemporary psychoanalysts have gone even beyond Jacobson. Most of Freud's ideas on this subject are now discarded or revised. The issue of penis envy, for example, is seen as a metaphor (Grossman & Stewart 1976).

Jacobson's reasoning leads her to conclude that the girl develops an earlier and much stronger superego than the boy. As early as the second year of life, with awareness of anatomical difference and the acquisition of gender identity, the little girl begins to identify with strength and, as a consequence of toilet training, with cleanliness. She becomes a good, clean, obedient little girl, transferring phallic strivings to her entire body instead of to her perceived-to-be inadequate genital. Her ego ideal becomes physical attractiveness. She acquires high moral values, devalues her mother somewhat, and turns to her father, thus making a heterosexual object choice. Later in life she need not, as Freud thought, remain fixated in this incestuous object relationship, but can resolve the oedipal conflict just as does the boy, out of love for the parent of the same sex which surmounts the rivalry. She is thereby able, at the phase-appropriate time, to choose a nonincestuous life partner.

Jacobson also makes an outstanding contribution to the psychology of depression. The roots of depression, she finds, lie in the contrast between wishful self-images and the image of a failing self. This is related to abandonment by object images, especially if that very severe form of object loss occurs before a separate identity is established.

Spitz

Spitz elaborates the process by which the ego becomes organized. Organization proceeds within the reciprocal relationship of the mother-child dyad in which communication takes place by means of affective interchanges. Once again we see that object relations theory and ego psychology are indivisible.

For analogy, Spitz borrows from embryology, where it is known that, before organization, transplanted tissue assumes the quality of the surrounding tissue. But after organization and specialization this is no longer possible because the tissue has acquired an "identity." Spitz suggests that the psyche undergoes analogous organization. This is one of the few discoveries in psychoanalytic theory construction that can be proven experimentally because each of the organizers has an observable indicator which demonstrates that a certain degree of organization has taken place. If organization fails, or is delayed, the indicator is absent at the phase-appropriate time.

An important contribution to a theory of object relations is Spitz's careful distinction between humans and some other animals. Humans are altricial—that is, they are incapable of providing for themselves for a long period after birth. Many animals are precocial—able to become relatively independent of the mother at or shortly after birth. Therefore, simple extrapolation from animal experiments is likely to be inaccurate. The first, very primitive form of object relationship in humans serves survival.

Integrating Spitz's findings with the thoughts of those who preceded him—Hartmann and Jacobson—one can understand the internal shifts that take place in the first weeks of life when self and object images, merged, of course, are acquired by affective experience, and how an embryonic ego begins to be organized.

It was Glover (1932) who proposed that the ego is formed out of "nuclei" which are established by affective experience. As similar nuclei accumulate, they cluster together to form "islands." These, as they proliferate, join together to form the "continent" or structure that is the ego. Although Freud had already indicated that the ego develops out of experience with the outside world, Glover's was the first intimation that this development is a form of organization.

The first indicator that organization has begun is the smiling response. Perception has shifted from within to the external world. Affect is linked with intentionality. The child can smile at a human face in motion because, in normal development, that configuration has become organized into a recognizable whole and is cathected with preponderantly positive experience. The smiling response indicates that a rudimentary organization exists and that social relations have begun.

At the next level of organization, the specific mothering person is recognized and distinguished from strangers. This is a large step in ego organization and in development of object relations, expanding the capacity to cathect object images and by newly acquired perceptual ability to distinguish one human face from another. This is how the infant makes a specific connection with the *libidinal object proper.*

At the third level of ego organization, semantic communication, a new and qualitatively different level of object relations is reached. Now the differentiating child has to communicate verbally, no longer by means of coenesthetic sensing which was characteristic of the more merged state. But speech alone is not in itself an indicator of organization. Almost everyone, even the mute psychotic on a narcissistic level of object relations, knows how to speak. The use of speech for semantic communication involves awareness that object images are separate from self-images, and includes the intention to communicate across ego boundaries. This will remain the principal mode of communication throughout life, with certain exceptions when there is a temporary and reversible merger for pleasure or for artistic creation (Kris 1952).

Synchronicity is stressed because of the crucial importance of the maintenance of homeostasis. There are *critical periods,* where there must be confluence of biological maturation with psychological development.

Spitz summarizes his concept of ego organization:

> The first of the organizers of the psyche structures perception and establishes the beginnings of ego. The second integrates object relations with the drives and establishes the ego as an organized psychic structure with a variety of systems, apparatuses, and functions. The third organizer finally opens the road for the development of object relations on the human pattern, that is, the pattern of semantic communication. This makes possible both the emergence of the self and the beginning of social relations on the human level. (1959:96–97)

Mahler

Mahler began her investigations with the study of psychosis in children (1951, 1953). She notes the severe disturbances in self and object relations in psychosis. This led her next to her landmark study of normal mother-child pairs in which she ascertains how normal development takes place within the dyadic experience. The results of that study have become the key to understanding normal development, pathological deviations, and pathogenic potential sometimes amenable to primary prevention. In addition, they pave the way for the elaboration of treatment techniques for the understructured personalities of children and adults. More than any other investigator, Mahler sheds light on the hitherto obscure areas of the so-called borderline and narcissistic pathologies.

She discovered that there are three major phases in early development and designates these as *autistic, symbiotic,* and *separation-individuation.* In her later work she describes separation-individuation not as a phase, but as a process with four subphases.

Spitz and Mahler established the pattern for future child observation to include psychoanalytic inference. Some accuse her of adultomorphic speculation (Kohut 1971), others contend that the psychoanalysis of adults is the only valid source of psychoanalytic inference. Most psychoanalysts, including Freud (1920b), believe that only the combined results of child observation and exploration of adult pathology can lead to deeper insights. To the extent that psychoanalysis as a theory is a science, it is to be noted that scientists welcome data from all sources.

Stern (1976), in light of his own observation of neonates and that of others (Brazelton & Robey 1965), challenges Mahler's finding that there is an autistic phase. Those studies do indeed show that the neonate responds to the outside world earlier than was heretofore believed. There are credible movie films and videotapes of infants who, soon after birth, respond selectively to the sound of the mother's voice and appear to imitate her mouth movements. But whether these behaviors do indeed prove that there is awareness of an object world so soon after birth remains in question. What is proven is that there is greater alertness and more response to stimuli than had previously been thought. We think that this calls for revision of the long-held belief that the neonate requires a high stimulus barrier, but we cannot conclude that self and object images exist at birth. This remains unproven, and given the developmental theory now available, it seems unlikely that such degree of organization can be present so early. Mahler (personal communication) points out that advances in technology make it possible to investigate minutiae of neonatal life that may lead to revision of her concept of an autistic phase, or alteration of her timetable, and may lead also to other conclusions. Closer observation of normal children suggests that Spitz's timetable also may require revision, but that does not invalidate his conclusions.

While the concept of an autistic phase may have to be reconsidered, there is no doubt that the next phase, symbiosis, is the basis for the child's progress into the object world. At that phase self and object images are joined for the purpose of accumulating essential self and object affective experiences. During symbiosis the experience of oneness constitutes a form of object relations in which the infant gains basic gratification that lasts a lifetime. It becomes the template for all future gratification as well as for empathy and love, and it is a point of temporary reversible regression at moments of pleasure. Where the capacity to enter the symbiotic unity is deficient because of inborn incapacity to extract from the environment, symbiotic fulfillment cannot be attained, and the child does not enter the object world. With that observation, Mahler provides insight into childhood psychosis and predisposition for psychotic pathology later in life.

This is the basis for our difference with the psychiatric view of the outbreak of psychosis as something similar to a physical illness that invades a healthy body. We refer instead to a psychotic structure, a predisposition to psychosis established in an inadequate symbiotic experience. Because of this, an individual can reach adolescence and even adulthood without overt psychotic manifestations, only to become overtly psychotic when external stress or the stress of developmental tasks is too great for the fragile structure. The stress of adolescence, long known to be "prime time" for schizophrenia to occur, results in "dementia praecox" where structure is already inadequate. The best analogies we can find in a medical model are the latent genetic potentials that do not always result in overt illness, and diseases such as syphilis where the individual appears to be healthy for many years before the overt outbreak of secondary and tertiary symptoms. In our view, healthy structure does not break down under ordinary conditions of life. For breakdown to occur where structure is adequate, there must be extraordinary trauma. (See also chapter 12.)

With her observation about the innate capacity to extract from the environment, Mahler dispels the commonly held idea of the schizophrenogenic mother. The endowment deriving from the undifferentiated matrix determines whether the infant can enter symbiosis. Without this capacity on the part of the infant, the mother's exertions are of little avail. Some infants, with unusual effort on the part of the mother, can be helped to extract somewhat, but principally it is the child who must play his or her part in using what the environment has to offer. In Mahler's own terms, the lion's share of adaptive processes rests with the infant, who is at a peak of adaptive capacity. We find in this some interesting implications for treatment, involving the "division of labor" between patient and therapist, which we shall elaborate upon.

Mahler alters object relations theory radically. The child cannot be regarded as a blank slate upon whom experience is etched. Object relations grow out of a reciprocal process in which the child, with his or her unique endowment, plays a dominant role. This suggests that object relations theory is far more than the simple action of the environment upon the child; it is infinitely more complex, involving action, reaction, and interaction.

Symbiosis, which was under the dominance of the libidinal drive, wanes as the aggressive drive comes into ascendancy to power the thrust into the separation-individuation process. In the normal family situation, the child's widening interest in the object world brings the father into that world; he joins the child's own separating tendency, luring the child out of symbiosis (Greenacre 1972). The mother, too, must gently nudge the child from the nest when she senses his or her readiness for a modicum of separation. Thus there are three factors that propel the child into the separation-individuation process—the ascendancy of the aggressive drive, which includes the need to exercise developing functions; the increasing interest in the larger object world with the father actively making that world interesting; and the mother's ability to relinquish her symbiotic need for the child when the child's need for separation becomes patent. The mother of symbiosis must become the mother of separation-individuation at the phase-appropriate time.

In the first subphase of the separation-individuation process—differentiation—the child begins to become aware of differences between self and object images. The second subphase—practicing—involves first quadrupedal and then bipedal locomotion, which enables the child to explore the wider world and to experience the affect, elation, that is so essential to establishment of self-esteem and willingness to venture. The next subphase—rapprochement—is ushered in by the child's increased awareness that he or she is alone, small, and vulnerable in a very large world. The ensuing separation anxiety causes one more return to "home base." This step, which is only apparently a backward one, is in fact a regression in the service of development. It must meet with the mother's welcome if the child is to move comfortably into the next subphase—on-the-way-to-object-constancy. If the rapprochement experience is less than satisfactory, the child experiences sharp disappointment. Mahler believes that this predisposes to depression.

The fourth subphase, on-the-way-to-object-constancy, is deliberately left open-ended because Mahler wishes to convey that there is no timetable for this process.

It is essential to emphasize that this is not a simplistic scheme of development that repeats in a sequential pattern. Our own concept of organization, which we shall elaborate upon throughout this work, precludes such systematization. Beyond that, the very nature of development, with its progressions, regressions, condensations, and distortions, suggests that even in the first round of development, when one phase and subphase does follow the other more rather than less sequentially, there are overlappings, regressions, and, above all, individual and unique elaborations of this basic developmental pattern.

G. Blanck and R. Blanck

G. Blanck (1966) became interested in the technical implications of ego psychology for the psychoanalysis of the structured personalities and for the psychotherapy of the understructured when ego psychology was regarded as merely interesting, but of not much technical value (Loewenstein 1951). This was the climate of the psychoanalytic world at that time, even though Hartmann had written on "Technical Implications of Ego Psychology" in 1951 and Kris' series of papers on technique appeared in 1956.

R. Blanck (1965) wrote about the greater value of individual treatment in psychotherapy when group treatment was in vogue. Using R. Blanck's (1967) clinical experience in marriage counseling in conjunction with burgeoning knowledge about ego psychology, we (1968) collaborated on a book on marriage which integrates contemporary ego psychology with psychoanalytic theory as a whole to show that marriage is a developmental phase with its phase-specific tasks. Among these are: another round in the continuing resolution of the oedipal conflict and diminution of oedipal strivings by choice of a nonincestuous partner of one's own generation; psychological as well as physical separation from primary objects; preparation for parenthood.

Our second book, *Ego Psychology: Theory and Practice,* is an outgrowth of our teaching at the Institute for the Study of Psychotherapy. Having had experience in curriculum planning for psychoanalytic training, we undertook to present a curriculum for the training of psychotherapists who were treating the understructured personalities without systematized techniques. Planned as a text in psychotherapy, this work summarizes the contributions of the major ego psychologists and elaborates techniques for treatment. In the theoretical part, the sequence of ego psychological theory construction is outlined and its integration with the main body of psychoanalytic theory is demonstrated. Until then, the complementarity of the works of the several ego psychologists had not been organized into a single body of knowledge.

Also in that book, Freud's (1912b) acceptance of resistance as the "best support" for treatment is reclaimed because some authors on technique (Fenichel 1941; Menninger 1958; Greenson 1967) tend to present resistance as an obstacle to the therapeutic endeavor. The concept of the benign climate, also proposed by Freud and emphasized by Sharpe (1950), is revived. A new model for descriptive developmental diagnosis which we had first presented in 1968 is revised, extended, and elaborated. The manner in which preverbal experience is reflected in the transference is described as a tool for the reconstruction of early life experience. Conflict as the sole cause of pathological formation lost its exclusivity by the addition of considerations of the conflict-free sphere and adaptation.

In *Ego Psychology II: Psychoanalytic Developmental Psychology* (1979), we go beyond synthesis of the works of others, offering new postulates derived from our own clinical experience. We remembered from our very early training that teachers were very careful to distinguish drive from affect, and we noted with some surprise that this distinction had become lost over the years. Psychoanalytic communications to this very day refer to the aggressive drive where what is meant is *hostility.* Even those who maintain that the affects are drive-borne are in error when they confuse the source with its derivative.

We reinvestigated Freud's writings on drive theory and found that, in his final statement on the drives (1940), he says that libido is the force that seeks to make connections and create ever-greater unities and that the aggressive drive is the force that seeks to undo connections and thus destroy. That the severing of connections is destructive reflects Freud's retention of the concept of a death instinct (1920a). The ego psychologists have shown that the severing of connection on one level of the developmental process leads to the resumption of connection at the next-higher level.

We also improve our diagnostic scheme by the addition of a *Fulcrum of Development,* with fourteen developmental features that are to be taken into account in arriving at a diagnosis for treatment purposes. We show that, at the turning point or fulcrum, which coincides developmentally with the rapprochement subphase, there is a shift from the interpersonal mode to the intrapsychic mode. Negotiations between self and object representations now take place within the ego rather than exclusively with the external object in reality. Conflict is intrasystemic as well as intersystemic. There is now capacity to use anxiety as a signal and to use complex defense mechanisms. This scheme enhances diagnostic understanding, not only of the structured personality, but of the understructured—those who have not fully completed the developmental tasks that lead to structuralization.

We reconsider the very important technical matter of transference. Following logically from our conclusions about structuralization, and using Mahler's discovery that prestructural life is interpersonal, we found in our clinical experience that the understructured patient attempts to use the therapist as a real more than as a transference object. We review the concept of interpretable transference, which applies where there is sufficient structure for the patient to have had relationships with primary objects which had attained a whole, separate status. We see this developmental phenomenon as responsible for the ability of such persons to displace onto the analyst in the process of psychoanalytic treatment. Those patients who had not negotiated the Fulcrum successfully are still in active negotiations with primary object representations. This does not constitute displacement from past to present; it is persistence of primary object need. We noticed in the treatment situation that such "transferences" are uninterpretable (but not immutable) because they are lived in the here and now. We describe pathology as the result of developmental lag, regression, or combinations of both. We distinguish normal narcissism from narcissistic pathology, defining the latter as a pathology of object relations resulting from an imbalance in cathexis of self and object representations.

Out of these considerations, we elaborate ego-building techniques for the understructured personalities within a therapeutic climate that affords opportunity for structuralization. We found, in our clinical work, that regardless of the traditional diagnostic categories into which they fell, some patients have so little capacity for reorganization that the prognoses are poor, while others, having a better capacity for reorganization, can improve considerably with therapeutic help. There are even a few understructured personalities who can, with appropriate treatment, acquire structure and become able to proceed to classical psychoanalysis of a true transference neurosis.

CHAPTER 2
THE SUPERORDINATE SUPEREGO

IF WE WERE to be guided by chronology, we would find it more orderly to discuss the ego before proceeding to consideration of the superego. In the chronology of the history of psychoanalytic theory construction, Freud evolved the concept of ego over many years of his work before he was able to introduce the concept of superego. In the chronology of developmental theory, the ego comes into being before the superego. Here, however, we reverse that order because we wish to build on the contributions of certain theorists, Jacobson in particular, who use the concept of superego to elaborate on Freud's thoughts about a superordinate structure.

These ideas remain scattered through the literature, much of them mentioned in passing while the authors focus on other themes. Thus are theoretical implications of major importance all but lost in parenthetical asides and footnotes. We extract those ideas from their relative obscurity in order to highlight the concept of superordinate structure beyond the structural theory. This brings theory to a new level of abstraction and will contribute, inevitably, to technical refinements.

Freud (1923) entitled his introduction of the structural theory *The Ego and the Id.* Yet a major portion of that work is devoted to definition and description of the superego. This is because, by 1921, in "Group Psychology and the Analysis of the Ego," he had already worked out his thoughts about the ego rather clearly and therefore used the 1923 work to elaborate on the tripartite theory as a whole. He defined superego as a differentiated grade within the ego, derived from the transformation of object cathexes into identifications. Here we see that, long before object relations were identified as a specific factor in theory construction, Freud was aware that, more than any other aspect of structure, the superego is dependent upon identifications, i.e., object relations, for its very formation.

The drives are regarded by most theorists as innate. An exception is Loewald (1980), who believes that the drives develop in interaction with the object. Jacobson follows Hartmann in maintaining that the drives arise from the undifferentiated matrix, and she adds that they separate out into libido and aggression under the auspices of adequate mothering.

The ego, according to Freud, arises from the id in contact with the external world. According to Hartmann, both ego and id arise out of an undifferentiated matrix. Hartmann also proposes that there is a conflict-free sphere of the ego which can develop, in certain respects, outside of object relations and outside of conflict. Of course such an ego would not be competent to negotiate with the object world because those functions that are dependent upon interaction with an object would have failed to develop. Nevertheless, there are individuals who are severely impaired structurally in the area of self and object relations, but who function with conflict-free capabilities. Such persons present an appearance of being able to get along in the world so long as their activities do not require consideration for others. But those with in-adequate superego development, the so-called psychopaths and socio-paths, do not possess the social, ethical, and moral values that can only be acquired by interaction between self and object images in the de-velopmental years. On this matter Freud says: "The effects of the first identifications made in earliest childhood will be general and lasting" (1923:31).

Theorists, even those who write as clearly as Freud, sometimes have to turn to the poets for more elegant explication. Freud quotes Goethe on identification: What thou hast inherited from thy fathers acquire it to make it thine.

Freud had to grope for understanding the "intaking" processes, working out his thoughts over several years. In 1917 he used the phrase "The shadow of the object fell upon the ego" (p. 249) to describe identification, viewing the process as a way of replacing lost objects. His thoughts in 1921 represent an advance from that earlier position as he began to think that identification also arises out of a new per-ception of a common quality shared with another person. By 1923 his ideas about identification link that process with superego formation. The superego, he says, originates in the first identification:

> one which took place while the ego was still feeble, and on the other hand it is the heir to the Oedipus complex, and has thus introduced the most momentous objects into the ego. (p. 48)

Despite Freud's attempts to gain greater clarity, there remains considerable confusion about the distinctions among the processes—identification, incorporation, introjection, and even internalization—despite clarification attempted by Schafer (1968), Loewald (1973a), and Meissner (1972, 1973, 1974, 1976). In our earlier writing (1974) we regarded internalization as the generic term for the "intaking" processes, with introjection and incorporation representing more primitive processes, while identification was thought to take place either on a higher level, or alongside those other processes. Some authors use *identification* interchangeably with these other terms. As we come to understand more about self and object relations, and especially about the transfer of the functions of representations of the object to representations of the self, the confusion is diminished because the very terms are rendered obsolete.

As terms as well as concepts, introjection and incorporation are especially flawed because they were conceived at a time before the radical change in thinking brought about by the introduction of the concept of mental images and representations. Consequently they retain a literal connotation; one tends to think of introjection of a part or whole real object, and of incorporation of a tangible idea, stricture, or prohibition. Even the term *identification*, while less literal, is confusing because it has been used in two different ways—as a mechanism of defense and as a normal developmental process. Hartmann and Loewenstein take a long step toward clarification of this matter by pointing out that "the role of identification depends, at least in part, upon the developmental level on which it takes place" (1962:52).

We propose that these processes are now more adequately described as the process whereby functions of the object representations are transferred to the self representations. This is an important aspect of structure building. (This is elaborated upon in chapter 7.) Here we illustrate this with the rather simple example of the young child beginning to be able to perform the daily tasks of dressing, eating, and bodily care. The child has learned these "functions" by observation of their performance by the object and, as physical capability matures, takes these functions over. But it is an oversimplification to regard this process as restricted to the realm of that which is easily observed. Functions such as values, affectively tinged attitudes, and other such less tangible aspects of the object representations are also transferred to the self representations. Here one can look for illustration to such matters as affects and attitudes toward the anal product, which become transferred to the self-images and are then reinforced by reaction-formation. Another illustration is that attitudes toward the self, acquired from attitudes of the object, become internalized in the forms of approved-of or disapproved-of self representations.

The transfer of functions of the object representations to the self representations proceeds as a continuous exchange from the beginning of the developmental march through all phases of the life cycle. It is an object relations theory *par excellence* because it recognizes the fact that there is object negotiation throughout life and allows for the influence of contemporary as well as primary objects.

Self-image and object image refer to specific mental processes that take place at given moments in development. Not only do they contain the concept of mental images rather than real persons, but they describe a time frame. An image becomes established when there is an instantaneous affective experience that creates it. As these images coalesce into more permanent structures, when self and object constancy are attained, we refer to them as representations to connote their stability (Lichtenberg 1975). It will be recognized that the idea of images becoming representations is analogous to Glover's concept of ego nuclei that accumulate with experience, with like nuclei coalescing into "islands."

On rereading Freud with the objective of tracing his evolving thoughts about the superego, its formation and its functions, we find reflection of the inevitable uncertainty inherent in theory construction. What is the psychic institution called superego? Is it the severe, moralistic, punishing voice of conscience and the vehicle for retribution, or is it a system of regulation—of self and object cathexis—of preservation of equilibrium and of self-esteem as well as object esteem? Is the superego a depersonified, observing agency separated from the ego, which, in extreme cases, provides hostile auditory and visual hallucination? Or is it a differentiated grade *within* the ego, heir to the Oedipus complex, which changes the lowest part of mental life into what is highest in the human mind?

What is the role and function of identification in superego development? Is it the defensive retreat incurred by the loss of object cathexis as in melancholia? Is it the agency which has selected only the parents' strictness and severity to abuse the helpless ego which is at its mercy? Or does it incorporate other, more loving aspects of the parents and, if so, by what means?

And is superego structure fixed only in early parental prohibitions? Was Freud (1923) correct in saying that later components only enter the ego? Or do they also enter the superego? Would it be more useful to distinguish superego components from superego as structure?

What is the role and function of the superego in neurosis? Is neurosis the result of a conflict between the demands of the id and the resistance of the ego created at the behest of the superego? Or is it the lagging of ego development behind libidinal development that is the essential precondition for neurosis? Are these the causes of the more severe pathologies? Is the Oedipus complex a consequence of psychological misinformation which tends to confuse triadic object relations and sexual wishes? And what is the role of the diphasic onset of sexuality?

Other questions are concerned with the function of reality testing which Freud attributed at times to the ego and at other times to the superego.

Superego is defined by Moore and Fine as:

A theoretical concept designating those psychic functions which, in their manifest expression, represent moral attitudes, conscience, and the sense of guilt. It results from the *internalization* of the ethical standards of society in which the person lives, and develops by *identification* with the attitudes of parents and other significant persons in the child's environment. Superego functions may be divided into two categories: (1) The protective and rewarding functions set up ideals and values that are grouped under the term *ego ideal*; (2) the critical and punishing functions which evoke the sense of guilt and the pangs of conscience. In the *structural theory*, the superego is one of the three component parts or systems of the *psychic apparatus. In neuroses, symptoms arise as compromises in the conflict between instinctual drives (id derivatives) and the forces seeking to forbid or restrain their expression (the superego). Such conflict is described as inter-systemic.* (1967:87)

This definition attempts to resolve some of the contradictions in the theory by ascribing to the superego both protective and rewarding functions, on the one hand, and critical and punishing functions, on the other. But it is restricted to consideration of intersystemic conflict only, thereby omitting consideration of the complexities of prestructural development.

Most theorists are in agreement that the superego is the heir to the Oedipus complex. Freud (1923) described it as a differentiated grade within the ego which arises out of the ego's struggle with the oedipal conflict. But the logic of a developmental point of view suggests that the superego cannot arise full-blown at that rather late time in development. Hartmann and Loewenstein (1962) clarify that issue by pointing out that there are genetic determinants of the superego that are formed before superego formation proper, but they emphasize that these are not early forms of superego. We (1979) elaborate on their concept of superego formation, borrowing the term *components* from them. Later, on a higher level of integration, these components become more fully organized and integrated into a more stable structure with a greater degree of constancy.

Jacobson agrees that the superego is formed from preoedipal forestages which consist of disconnected components that originate in self and object imagery of different instinctual and ego stages and levels. She says:

The imagistic components in which the superego originates will mature, change with regard to their content, and assume abstract qualities. Only at this stage can selected ideal, directive, prohibitive, disapproving, and approving parental traits and attitudes and parental teachings become constructively correlated and gradually blended into a consistent, organized set of notions. (1964:126)

and:

The superego will then, in turn, achieve the final solution of the incestuous problem and further promote the process of ego maturation, the growth and

organization of personal relations and identification, and the establishment
of a solid defense system. (Ibid.)

and:

> There is a tremendous step from the simple moral logic of castration fear,
> of fear of punishment and hope for reward, to the abstract moral level of a
> superego which has expanded from the taboo of incest and murder to a set
> of impersonal, ethical principles and regulations for human behavior.
> (p. 127)

Freud's use of the term *ego ideal* as synonymous with superego is also
ambiguous. Some suggest that the ego ideal is a function of the superego. Jacobson describes it as a special area within the superego where
tension between the ego ideal and the wished-for self-image can create
problems in self-esteem. Milrod proposes that

> one could define the ego ideal as a more or less stable substructure in the
> superego, made up of the moral and ethical values meaningful to that in-
> dividual. (1982:99)

That processes of differentiation and integration are interwoven, leading to next-higher levels of differentiation and integration in an endless
chain, is an organizing principle that tends to reconcile the many
uncertainties and discrepancies in theory construction. This concept,
contributed by Hartmann and Spitz in the main, is of major importance
in providing some cohesion, which prevents theoretical groping from
becoming chaotic. Of equal importance, although on another level of
abstraction, is the fact that the human being functions as a complete,
albeit complex, whole. This implies that there is usually a balance, no
matter how tenuous and temporary, of all of the forces that are brought
to bear upon the individual at a given moment. There is an entire
spectrum of possibilities which differ greatly in quality, but are all
designed to restore balance. This ranges from neurotic compromise
formation on the one extreme, to decompensation and fragmentation
on the other.

Placing the matter of balance at the center of consideration renders
irrelevant questions about which institution is operative at a given
moment. Sometimes we are forced to think of the operation of a par-

ticular element in isolation from the whole, but this is for heuristic purposes. Whether a phenomenon emanates from the ego or the super-ego is sometimes useful to consider in working on the clinical detail of a particular situation, but even when so dividing the psyche in order to consider functions of one structure or another, the clinician as well as the theorist bears the whole person in mind.

Freud (1912b) warned against trying to fit patients into a particular frame of reference. He advocated that the clinician employ evenly sus-pended attention so that one may hear and tolerate complexities and contradictions even when such a stance goes counter to the understand-able human tendency to find order and certainty in the material under observation. Probably one of the most demanding requirements of the practitioner of the "impossible" profession of psychoanalysis is the abil-ity to tolerate uncertainty, for only by that means can one grope toward true understanding of the patient and toward new discoveries in theory construction. Uncertainty is only perturbing where the clinician feels he must "know" even though much remains unknown and unknowable. This is as relevant in relation to clinical practice as it is to theory construction.

The superego, like the ego, is a product of multiple functions and complex processes of differentiation and integration, as are all other aspects of psychic organization. We need not be dismayed, therefore, that superego theory at this juncture can provide nothing more than a glimpse of a not fully understood structure that arises from not fully understood components which, in turn, come about from not fully understood processes of internalization. However much we value struc-tural theory, it can become a morass of poorly defined institutions and systems at odds with each other if we demand utter clarity and spec-ificity about each institution. Thus, while the study of the individual agencies is of heuristic value, the fact is that the structural components, like the disputed child before King Solomon, cannot be divided.

In contemporary thought the struggle to conquer oedipal wishes is a developmental requirement for both sexes. The superego as heir to the Oedipus complex is the outcome of struggle in which superego components form an alliance with the ego against the oedipal wishes. As allies, ego and superego gain strength one from the other, and both gain strength from the exercise of function. Unified by the struggle, the superego components cohere to emerge as a distinct structure. That is the structural aspect. On the object relations side, love for the parent of the same sex overcomes rivalry. This aspect of superego formation, first proposed by Jacobson, was elaborated upon by Schafer. He finds that

> there is a loving and beloved aspect of the superego. It represents the loved and admired oedipal and preoedipal parents who provide love, protection, comfort, and guidance, who embody and transmit certain ideals and moral structures more or less representative of their society, and who, even in their punishing activities, provide needed expressions of parental care, contact, and love. (1960:186)

Jacobson says:

> In summary, the superego introduces a safety device of the highest order, which protects the self from dangerous internal instinctual stimuli, from dangerous external stimuli, and hence from narcissistic harm. (1964:133)

and:

> I have stated that the *centralized, regulating power of the superego* can modify the course of the self- and object-directed discharge processes in a generalized way. (Ibid.; italics ours)

When the superego becomes a system in its own right, it is a functional unit consisting of ethical principles and regulations for behavior.

Jacobson enumerates the functions of the superego, adding some that suggest superordinate qualities. From this we derive the thought that it is useful for theory construction to conceive of structure superordinate to the agencies of the structural theory. She describes:

1. A regulatory and direction-giving function.
2. Guiding and self-critical functions.
3. An enforcing function.
4. Provision of a new affective experience—guilt.

These do not differ from the generally accepted functions of the superego as described by Freud. To them, however, Jacobson adds:

5. Maintenance of stable balance in drive energy.
6. Regulation of drive discharge.
7. Cathexis of self and object representations.
8. Regulation of self-esteem by maintaining harmony between moral codes and ego manifestations.
9. Governing of moods.
10. Regulation of the entire ego state.
11. Development and maintenance of a coherent, consistent defense organization.

Functions 5 through 11 are not usually regarded as superego functions. In fact, it may be argued that many, if not all, are traditionally thought to be ego functions. We believe that Jacobson intended to convey that these functions are of an administrative nature. For example, the defensive function has always been ascribed to the ego. But in describing a coherent, consistent defense organization, Jacobson refers, not to defenses nor to defense mechanisms, but rather to organization. We find this to be the key to the description of functions that go beyond 1 through 4. These are functions that pertain to organization and administration, as contrasted with execution on an operational level. In fact, Jacobson is describing an agency that oversees the entire ego state. She does not mention that her thinking is related to Freud's thoughts about a superordinate ego. Yet it is fair to speculate that she was familiar enough with Freud's work to have absorbed his idea that there are structures beyond the structural theory.

CHAPTER 3
THE SUPERORDINATE EGO

IN 1921, shortly before he proposed the structural theory, Freud had begun to think about structure in the broad sense, as well as in the narrower sense of tripartite structure. But he put that aside, perhaps with the intention of developing it further at some later time. Although he did not return to it, his fundamental idea of structure that is superordinate to the agencies of the structural theory was taken up by others. We have shown how Jacobson applied that concept to superego theory. Here we continue to elaborate that theme by showing the advantages to theory construction of entertaining the idea of a superordinate ego.

Tracing the history of the evolution of the concept of *ego* in Freud's thought, Hartmann (1964) shows that it began with Freud's early (1900) mention of counterforce or censorship (later to become ego and superego). By 1921, Freud had already said:

> Let us reflect that the ego now enters into the relation of an object to the ego ideal which has developed out of it, and that all of the interplay between an external object and the *ego as a whole,* with which our study of the neuroses has made us acquainted, may possibily be repeated upon this new scene of action within the ego. (p. 130; italics ours)

Although his chief objective here is to work out the relationship between ego and ego ideal (superego), not entirely incidentally, he introduces a thought about an ego as a whole. Elaboration of this germ of an idea was postponed or deflected because the seminal nature of the structural theory led theorists to focus their attention upon the ego and superego as Freud describes them in 1923. We note:

The propulsive power of the structural theory is such that we have yet to see the end of its enormous potential for theory construction. After almost 50 years, its thrust still extends far into the future. (1972:668)

Theory construction in the several decades after 1923 does indeed follow the direction provided by the structural theory. It became fashionable, probably because it is so convenient, to resort to military analogies. Freud set the pattern by referring to armies. The positioning of the main bodies and their forward patrols is a way of describing fixation and of cautioning the analyst not to be misled when he or she notes clinically that certain aspects of development have proceeded beyond the "main army." Anna Freud's work on the defensive function of the ego falls quite easily into that descriptive style. Because it deals with conflict and defense, military metaphor became the order of the day. A defending ego fends off "attacks" by "neighboring powers" who are "invading" the "surrounding territory." When Wilhelm Reich's work enjoyed a short-lived popularity, there was talk of character "armor," in German, *Panzer*—a word which was to become so infamous in the military vocabulary of World War II. We, too, have not been immune to the militarization of psychoanalysis, having employed the metaphor of a "forward artillery observer" to refer to the patient whose task it is to correct the "salvos fired" by the therapist. Conflict theory does make these military terms appear irresistible. But we shall show that, although conflict is an aspect of the structural theory, it is not the whole of it.

A few theorists allude now and then to a unifying or executive function. Among these are Rangell (unpublished paper) and Glover, who says:

> No mental event can be described in terms of instinct alone, of ego structure alone, or of functional mechanism alone. . . . Each event should be estimated also in terms of . . . the relation of the *total ego* to its environment. It suggests that the most practical (clinical) criterion weakness or strength should be in terms of adaptation. (1943:310–311; italics ours)

In 1959 Spitz returned theory to consideration of the ego as a whole with his concept of organization. His observations led him to describe how the psyche becomes organized on ever-higher levels of integration. The first organizer involves recognition of the existence of an object world, the second refers to the establishment of the specific libidinal object, and the third to the immense widening of the scope of object relations marked by the acquisition of semantic communication and the capacity to say no. He also introduces the concept of a force field:

> From the side of the psyche, the establishment of memory systems and the displacement of energy along memory traces have introduced the possibility of a delay of drive discharge. With this the *systematic direction* of drives and their coordination and interdependence become possible. This is then what we mean by the organization of a force field in the psyche. (1959:25; italics ours)

The idea of a force field is so useful to a unitary theory because it allows room for the possibility that id requirements and ego functioning are not always in conflict but also operate, at times, as an integrated unit. Even at very early degrees of differentiation, there are aspects of drive and ego functions that are already organized into a cohesive albeit primitive unit of behavior, of function, and therefore of structure.

In describing the second organizer, Spitz says: "A metapsychological exploration of these manifestations leads to the assumption that a major change has taken place in the central steering organization (1959:38). The term *central steering organization* refers to the organized direction of energy, affect, and drive, conducted by already existing structures, as well as increased capacity for comprehension of external reality. The psychic systems themselves are being coordinated and brought into harmony with the surround by that superordinate structure, even as they are being differentiated.

Jacobson's thoughts about the functions of the superego are undoubtedly influenced by thoughts about superordinate structure. It becomes evident in retrospect that both Jacobson and Spitz are influenced by Freud's ideas about an ego as a whole. This thread is taken up by Loewald (1978), who is quite clear about Freud's intention to introduce the concept of a superordinate ego that differs from the ego of structural theory. Loewald says:

> Freud at times spoke, in reference to this ego, as the gesamt Ich "the ego as a whole" when he wanted to distinguish it from the ego considered as counterpart to id and superego. (1978:504)

We regard the *central steering organization* and the *superordinate ego* as synonymous. In our earlier work (1979) we referred to it as the *organizing process,* although it appeared then as a function of the ego of the structural theory.

Now we are able to elaborate. The organizing process creates systems formed out of repetitive experience, that become more rather than less stable, after an initial period of transience. Hartmann (1939) designates these systems as *automatisms,* and observes that they are essential for conservation of psychic energy. In an extension of the idea of automatisms we suggest that they evolve through repetitive prototypical experiences which achieve coherent organization by using specific pathways, programs, defenses, and adaptations to attain ever-greater stability. They consist of physical acts, defensive arrangements, memory structures, integrative functions, and, above all, the systems that arise out of interaction of innate endowment with nurturing environment. These are the ego systems which evolve out of daily experience.

Included there are those programmed patterns of relatedness to self and others called *object relations* which, of course, involves transference phenomena. These have their roots in the earliest period of life characterized by coenesthetic reception (Spitz). Spitz makes the important and much-overlooked observation that this mode of functioning continues to direct our feelings and actions in powerful but, of course, unconscious ways *throughout life.* Automatisms (Hartmann), as well as coenesthetic functioning, are organized into a unity, for they consist of fundamental aspects of object experience. Thus they maintain connection with our primary object experiences, constituting our very roots. Persons lacking such connection are disoriented within themselves and in their object worlds.

Inclusion of the concept of a superordinate ego in our metapsychology enables us also to explain the processes that involve adaptation in the broader and narrower senses as proposed by Hartmann. The ego functions of the well-enough endowed infant burgeon and change radically as development proceeds in an environment that is sufficiently nurturing, for it is the combination of innate and environmental factors that is involved in adaptation. Under such favorable conditions the superordinate ego can undertake the broader task of integrating specific individual functions that have become established and operative, while the adaptive capacity in the narrower sense continues to establish new systems to meet the needs of new daily experience. This describes a two- (or more) tiered structural apparatus and functional capacity which is completely consonant with the structural theory. Where there are less than optimal conditions for adaptation, as Spitz (1945) discovered in his study of hospitalism, the functioning of the central steering organization is limited to attempts to ensure survival and can even fail in that function. In accord with the dual drive theory, the so-called instinct of self-preservation is now subsumed under the libidinal drive. But if we consider it, for a moment, as an important aspect of that drive, it becomes evident that self-preservation is almost synonymous with adaptation in the human infant and is inextricably bound up with object connection.

Perhaps all will become clearer if restated in terms of a specific function of the superordinate ego. The quickening of individual ego functions which initiate the functioning of adaptive mechanisms on the narrower level of immediate experience is accomplished within the context of developing capacities on a broader level of adaptation. This involves modifying, altering, expanding, minimizing, or even dispensing with existing functions in order to meet newly developing drive and ego requirements. The superordinate ego has the global task of bringing the various structures together into some cohesive and coherent form, and also of assuring that they conform with drive needs and with the requirements of reality. How competently this superordinate organization functions is determined by the combination of innate capacities and early experience. The superordinate ego is essential for performance of the task of bending individual functions to the broader adaptive purposes that serve the entire organization. It makes the difference between rigid structures which become maladaptive and those which can address the exigencies of reality more flexibly, a matter we shall exploit in our consideration of the several modes of transference (chapter 8).

Where circumstances are optimal the superordinate ego uses the systems that are already in existence in a flexibly adaptive fashion to fit together organism and nurturing environment. Where they are less than optimal, it facilitates regression to fixation points that are relatively safer. Thus it strives always for preservation of the organism by resolution of conflict and favoring of ongoing developmental processes. Optimal resolution, which may range from neurotic compromise to regressive retreat, or to the restitutive attempts in psychosis, depends upon the following factors:

1. The innate capacity of the individual.
2. The quality of the nurturing environment.
3. The efficiency of the multitiered systems that have become organized.
4. The magnitude of the environmental impact.

The superordinate ego organizes the earliest systems. Instinct, drive, physical apparatus, psychological purpose, in any combination, are brought into coherent organization. And when systems have become organized, it remains the function of the superordinate ego to oversee the stability of the arrangement within the turmoil of radical change. For example, when the function of memory, in the neonate, has expanded to the point where the gestalt of the human face is connected with relief of organismic distress, another ego function—anticipation— is quickened. But this development is not simply linear. There is qualitative difference, marked by a new level of integration. That, too, must change as increasingly higher and more complex levels of object relations are reached.

In the succeeding few months of life, the combining of experience to create new structures is an ongoing process that increases exponentially. The smiling response appears as the child recognizes the configuration of the full human face in motion, connoting the beginning of nonspecific object connection. As libidinal drive requirements to unite enhance perceptive capacity, that first organizer gives way to the second. Then the child no longer smiles at strangers, but reserves cathexis for the "libidinal object proper" (Spitz). By then, in good enough circumstances, the superordinate ego is no longer immediately involved with survival. The need for object connection, propelled by libidinal drive, is implemented by the existence of structures that, by this time of life, include a higher level of perception, cognition, accumulation of visual data, and increased memory storage capacity. It is these that contribute to the alteration of the three-month program in favor of cathexis of the specific object. Thus the next-higher organizer of the psyche, stranger anxiety, is established. This is how an earlier "program" undergoes modification.

Even as change is taking place, however, much is retained from before. Spitz designated this process as *cumulation*. Cumulated systems come into being as reality testing forces the alteration of patterns of object relations.

We think of the superordinate ego, then, as the executive agency of the psyche which has the ultimate function that Hartmann regards as more important than adaptation—namely, fitting together. Much that we describe here has always been tacitly accepted in earlier conceptualizations. Nunberg's (1931) thought is the somewhat narrower one of a synthetic function. Broader conceptualizations of the same basic theme (Hartmann) allude to an integrating function, and on a still-broader level, an organizing function. Although these accord well with Freud's definition of ego as coherent organization, they are constricted when bound within the confines of the structural theory of 1923. To assign such functions to a superordinate structure not only relieves the individual agencies of burden, but also makes it possible to visualize harmonious unification of the entire psychic structure, even when it is racked by conflict and change. This concept also makes it less necessary to ponder about whether to attribute a given function to id, to ego, or to superego, or even to ego ideal. While it continues to remain useful to examine the parts of the whole heuristically, excessive focus on the separate parts detracts from the fact that physical organism and psychic structure are parts of a unitary whole. The superordinate ego maintains that unity at all times, in conflictual, developmental, regressive, and progressive states, for the organism is never at rest.

CHAPTER 4
THE NATURE OF STRUCTURE

THE TERM *structure* is commonplace in psychoanalytic theory. As indicated by its frequent appearance in the literature, the functioning of structures has always been part of psychoanalytic conceptualizations of mental processes. The tripartite structure—id, ego, and superego—is so-called "because of the relative constancy of their objectives and consistency in modes of operation" (Moore & Fine 1967:86). Rapaport and Gill define structure as configuration with a slow rate of change in that cathexis is not dissipated. They add that "structures are configurations within which, between which and by means of which mental processes take place" (1959:803). These definitions refer to the fixed nature, the stability, of structure.

The terms *structure* and *configuration* are tautologies. They provide no frame of reference for understanding the means by which mental processes take place. The concept of cathexis, however, does provide a direction. It represents an investment of energy bound to drive need, which is the propellant for cathexes. Drives require an object for discharge. Drive need, object "seeking," object "finding," and drive discharge all quicken ego functions and lay down pathways for these to be exercised. Memory, more volitional vocalization, anticipation, and the like are thereby initiated by experience. These have to be provided by the mothering person in the beginning because the neonate's ability to seek and find is limited to the rooting reflex. Upon quickening there is a shift, as the neonate acquires a relatively greater degree of autonomy by the exercise of function.

That there are id, ego, and superego does not refer to the paradigm of structure—transference—which is never absent from the treatment situation. Freud recognized this by designating it as one of the two fundamental components of the psychoanalytic situation, the other being resistance. The concepts of structure and transference are inextricably intertwined with each other and with object relations. Transference phenomena reflect the existence of patterned forms of organization of memory and affect which exert lasting influence upon responses to other persons. At times such responses appear to be consonant with reality; at other times, even though they are inconsistent with reality in varying degrees, the pattern, having been established in early object experience, does not alter. That drive need can overpower judgment (love is blind) has been recognized for centuries. Patterns, therefore, may be said to possess an enduring quality which tends to remain constant and to acquire the status of structure by virtue of that constancy.

Edgcumbe also recognizes that. She says:

> Another set of core assumptions . . . is concerned with the role of enduring psychological and physiological tendencies to react to specific stimuli with individually specific patterns of cognitive, emotional, behavioral and physiological responses. These are partly inborn, partly learned, and are subject to modification and self-control. Developmental and environmental factors, especially those occurring during early development, help to shape future patterns. (1984:138)

Current discoveries about the development of object relations provide a broadened perspective for extension of knowledge about psychic structure. These discoveries were not available to Freud when (1914b) he thought that narcissistic structures are untreatable because the analyst could have no effective entrée. The avenue of connection to the narcissistic person is so distant, Freud believed, that it could only be glimpsed from afar. The transference neuroses, on the other hand, were deemed to be treatable precisely because the person of the analyst could be cathected, albeit in displaced form. But Freud came close to the modern understanding of the narcissistic arrangement when he reflected upon the fact that the prolonged dependence of the human infant has a decisive effect upon psychic structure. He touches here upon the impact of object experience and the formation of object relations.

Psychic structure is so complex that diagnosis from the object relations component alone results in reductionism. It is too simple to say that narcissistic formations are caused by failure in symbiotic connection in the first months of life. It is equally simplistic to say that the opposite of narcissism—symbiotic psychosis—is the result of failure to separate from the primary object; and that the middle ground is occupied by experience in normal symbiosis and separation-individuation processes. The oversimplification becomes more obvious as we take into account the fact that those who survive infancy have in some way experienced the human "touch"; there is always a degree of object cathexis that is a part of structure.

Glover's theory of ego development, useful as it is, remains abstract and metaphoric, bringing us no closer to specific knowledge of the actual process of structuralization. We have no way of visualizing an "island of experience" in the psyche except by concretization, nor can we account for how and why these "islands" coalesce except by ascribing such a process, as we do with so many unexplainable phenomena, to the synthetic function (Nunberg 1931). But Glover does provide information about component elements. These include affect and experience, the latter implying the existence of the ego function of memory.

Rapaport comments on our meager understanding of structure. He says:

> In psychoanalytic theory, structure plays such a crucial role that as long as the propensities and changes of psychological structure cannot be expressed in the same dimensions as psychological processes, dimensional quantification is but a pious hope. In other words, the study of the process of psychological structure formations seems to be the prime requisite for progress towards dimensional quantification. We must establish how processes turn into structures, how a structure once formed, changes, and how it gives rise to and influences processes. (1959:98–99)

To address the question of how structure is formed we refer to some phenomena of infant life. Because of data provided by recent infant observation it is now appropriate to think that some sort of primitive negotiation with the external object begins at birth. As has been pointed out, especially by Mahler, object negotiations are interpersonal in the early months of life.

Feeding has usually been regarded as the first interpersonal experience between the neonate and the mothering person. Some modern obstetrical techniques involve arranging darkened rooms and placing the neonate upon the mother's abdomen to cushion the entry into the extrauterine world. These practices are based on an assumption that experience with the external world begins even before feeding. But there is no question that the feeding experience becomes the earliest repetitive experience.

The neonate cries because of organismic distress caused by hunger. The sound of approaching footsteps, repeated forty or more times per week, registers in the auditory realm. This is followed almost immediately by the arrival of the mothering person, and immediately after that, by relief from hunger. The repeated appearance of the mother in coincidence with relief produces long-lasting consequences for object relations. Here are three, possibly four, disparate "islands of experience"—sound, arrival of "someone," relief, and possibly a rudimentary sense of time—which coalesce into a larger structure. The indicator that this has taken place is the qualitative alteration of the hunger cry and the quantitative change in decibel level as footsteps are heard approaching. A distinct and specific pathway involving both neurological and psychological components has been established, similar to a program in a computer. The change in the cry is the indicator that the following component elements have coalesced: memory traces, affect, anticipation, auditory reception, and alteration of drive discharge mechanism on the narrow level of adaptation, and capacity to combine all these disparate elements into a unit on the broad level. Thus, even at the beginning of life, the infant already demonstrates an ability to organize multiple factors.

To understand the operative internal mechanisms, one has to consider that uterine life is characterized by constant automatic regulation. So far as is known, the fetus experiences little or no disequilibrium. Birth disrupts the "automatic" support system and demands of the organism that it take over regulatory functions. The human infant is poorly equipped for that task. Unlike some lower animals, the infant has to "learn" how to regulate the organismic distress first experienced upon entry into extrauterine life.

Ability to regulate is acquired slowly and, even with optimal assistance from the outside, is established with wide variation in competence and rate from one infant to another. The rooting reflex leads the infant to the nipple and has as its purpose restoration of the equilibrium disturbed by hunger. But it is a poor instrument because it is random at first. The infant experiences distress in varying degrees until the nipple is securely captured. Only when the rooting reflex is joined by the ego function of anticipation does it become more reliable. Even then, if relief is delayed beyond the scope of the anticipatory function, the infant cannot stop crying when the nipple is inserted, as Spitz (1965) notes.

The cry begins as a reflexive act, possibly triggered by the need to supply oxygen in a new fashion. There are many variables among infants in the ability to "accept" external assistance in establishing regulatory systems. As the reflexive cry elicits response, a connective pathway (memory) begins to be laid down, probably a dawning awareness of cause and effect. The cry brings auxiliary assistance in the struggle to achieve regulation. The infant, however, cannot perceive this assistance as auxiliary.

Originally reflexive, the cry now has acquired the status of a function, is cathected as an instrument, and becomes volitional. But regulation of distress is not yet a goal; only the function of the cry is at first cathected. Functions have to be exercised, and so it often appears to the observer that the infant cries for the sake of crying. This, of course, is too simplistic. The function of the cry remains cathected until new solutions or programs are found to replace it. And in the final analysis, crying—our first mechanism for survival—is never entirely superseded by the newer programs, and is resorted to in times of distress throughout life.

Gradually the magical properties of the cry have to become decathected in order for the cry to acquire an object-related function. This has to be described with great caution; it would be incorrect to think that there are object images in the very first weeks of life. One can only speak vaguely of a dimly perceived "outside." Thus, it may be more correct to describe this as a shift from cathexis of the cry "for its own sake" to cathexis of a goal—assistance in the struggle to establish a reliable regulatory system.

This new aspect of the cry as a function establishes a connective pathway only to the extent that the function succeeds. That is a factor not only of the quality of the external response but also of the infant's capacity to process it, to use the response as an auxiliary regulatory aid. Here the capacity to extract from the environment is operative long before symbiotic unity is entered, and undoubtedly prepares for symbiosis. This thought supports our view of the first weeks of life as preparation for symbiosis rather than as autism or primary narcissism. It is a time when infant and mothering person seek a comfortable fitting together. The reciprocal relation between the organism and its environment is one of continuous struggle and adjustment. Seen this way, symbiosis represents the success of that adjustment.

Another effect of the gradual decathexis of the magical properties of the cry and of supplanting it with cathexis of the cry as object-related and goal-related function is the beginning of anxiety tolerance. At this point in development one cannot speak of a frustration-disappointment sequence, but only of a distress–loss of equilibrium sequence. The ingredients of a growth-promoting process moving toward development of anxiety tolerance include favorable experiences, increasing cathexis of the function, and increased reliance upon the possibility of favorable outcome which ultimately leads to object comprehension.

What does it take to enable the infant to seek new solutions instead of continuing to rely upon earlier programs? The forward progression of psychological development is seriously disrupted by loss of equilibrium and results in regression to organismic distress. The acquisition of ever-higher thresholds for tolerance of anxiety and frustration, and the ever-increasing capacity to limit regression, enable the infant to create more flexible and more complex programs.

In the succeeding few months of life, combining of experience to produce new and ever more elaborate and more complex structures continues and increases exponentially. To illustrate: as development proceeds, libidinal drive requirements to unite enhance perceptive capacity by propelling the infant toward the libidinal object proper. The first organizer gives way to the second. Then the child no longer smiles at strangers, but reserves cathexis for that specific object (Spitz). Here the adaptive function has led the infant into symbiosis. Entry into the first subphase of the separation-individuation process takes the individual a long step in the direction of autonomous functioning while, paradoxically, the symbiotic mode of seeking connection persists and is even enhanced by stranger anxiety. There is a taste of both the desirability of, and anxiety attendant upon, separation. An earlier "program" has undergone modification. But we know that this earlier program—the smiling response—is altered only if there is good enough development. In some unfortunate instances the smile, if it appears at all, remains unspecific because it is fixated in the symbiotic mode; the libidinal object proper does not become established. Such severe failure in development may be caused by environmental failure or by innate defect.

As innumerable structures ("programs") are being created and are attaining constancy and stability after an initial transient stage, the superordinate ego operates to bring the various functional structures into coherence and harmony, a goal that is achieved sometimes to a greater and sometimes to a lesser degree. When it is to a lesser degree the separate ego components will be in intrasystemic conflict. This extends Freud's and Jacobson's ideas about superordinate structure. It modifies only slightly Hartmann's (1939) concept of adaptation and it accords precisely with Hartmann's concept of adaptation as occurring in both the broader and the narrower senses.

Structure, then, may be understood to consist of a many-layered series of "programs," maintained and organized into coherent form by an executive apparatus, the superordinate ego. To try to convey the meaning of structure by means of the metaphor "programs" seems to us to be particularly apt, because that concept, borrowed from the computer world, implies that there are fixed forms of organized behavior which run off at a given signal. It also describes the existence of the patterned forms of negotiations which are established between the self representations and the object representations, namely object relations. And it is, of course, the source of transference repetition. These "programmed" sequences of negotiations with the object world begin at birth, as soon as the internal apparatus develops the capacity to process input. Random experiences, unless of particular significance or impact, would not be programmed, but the daily repetitious events would produce, sooner or later, stereotyped behavioral forms. This is the process whereby negotiations between newborn and primary object, interpersonal at first, become internalized, initially as isolated programs (islands) and then as clusters of programs which ultimately become integrated on higher levels of complexity and effectiveness.

We have described here a somewhat more detailed explanation of the process described by Hartmann (1939) as differentiation and integration. Hartmann's very definition of differentiation, the specialization of a function, refers to the establishment of a specific pathway for a mental operation. It is that which we are here designating as a program.

Such programs, initially created within the infant-mother matrix, seem to begin with preliminary forms that, it is speculated, are products of imprinting and reflexive processes. Within a few weeks, innate potential begins to process environmental input. Then increasingly autonomous programs are created. When this occurs, a new level of integrative effort is required and becomes essential for ongoing growth. For the daily experiences, simple programs will continue to suffice. For example, the young infant continues to smile at any configuration of the human face in motion, and not in profile. But the ongoing march of development demands the capacity to alter this program to accord with newly developed skills and needs. Thus, the adaptive structures formed on the narrow level of daily needs and experiences require a broader overview, calling into functional operation processes on a broader level of adaptation. It is here that the functioning of the superordinate ego must enter the process because the narrower structures cannot execute these broader tasks. This turn in mental processing is repeated again and again as development proceeds.

To recapitulate: the earlier structures consist of various internalizations, more primitive forms of defense, early forms of connection with objects and object images. These constitute the very warp and woof of the material of which transference manifestations are created. These are the component elements, not only of the transferences—they also represent early forms of object relations. When these component elements elude the efforts of the ego-as-a-whole (the superordinate ego), whose function it is to bring all the individual programs into coherence and harmony with each other and with reality, residual programs remain in effect, producing transference phenomena and forms of object negotiation less in tune with reality.

The existence of psychotic structure clearly indicates that, while programs of ego functions such as motility, speech, organization of perception, and the like have been successfully established, the overall task of the superordinate ego has failed in its purpose of bringing specific functions into accord with reality. The psychotic paranoid individual is arrested by a program which reflects his view of a hostile object world. The schizophrenic will grossly misperceive external reality, and will try to fit it together with the unalterable programs of his inner world, programs which have not been modified by the superordinate ego.

This view has been forced upon us by empirical experience in which an otherwise unaccountable mix of adaptive structures coexist side by side with severely pathological ideation. So-called normal functioning can proceed alongside extraordinarily magical thinking. Schreber, for example, lived for many years as a useful member of society until he regressed into totally psychotic ideation. We describe our view of psychotic structure in chapters 1 and 12, where we challenge the position that psychosis can break out where structuralization has proceeded normally.

CHAPTER 5
REALITY TESTING

THE MAJOR FUNCTION of the superordinate ego is to bring already established structures into harmony with each other and with reality. We have seen that, especially with regard to object perception, total success of this harmonious objective is not attainable. While the development of reality testing constitutes an essential aspect of the process of structuralization, the extent to which perception of reality approaches "true reality" varies from one individual to another, depending as it does upon the nature, quality, and level of object relations established. Acquisition of reality testing is strongly influenced by the earliest reception processes, which are global in nature and are least amenable to mutation. The very existence of transference phenomena in the clinical situation affirms the fact that, in all structures, reality testing, especially with regard to object perception, is highly subjective.

Hartmann knew this when he said, "The healthy adult's mental life is probably never quite free of the denial and replacement of some reality by fantasy formation" (1939:18). We would amend this slightly by adding that fantasy formation does not consist of "pure" fantasy but must include in its core past experiences which have become organized into programs, and have become modified and fitted into contemporary experience in some seemingly rational fashion.

Spitz also alludes to the influence of earliest experience upon later capacity for reality testing. Describing the effects of the coenesthetic organization, he says:

> The coenesthetic organization continues to function throughout life, powerfully, one might say, as the wellspring of life itself even though our Western civilization has fitted a silencer on its manifestations. (1965:45)

While Spitz is referring here to underlying affective potential, his message that the conenesthetic organization "plays a momentuous determining role in our feelings, our thinking, our actions" (*ibid.*) may be applied to those early experiences that continue to live in the present in transference manifestations which the superordinate ego has not succeeded in rendering totally consonant with reality.

To be accurate, one should refer only to perception of reality, rather than reality testing, since reality testing remains subjective and is readily modified by the emotional state of the moment. This idea was well conceptualized by Schafer when he coined the term "visions of reality" (1970). The practicing infant can get very upset with his mother who protectively restrains him from running out into a heavily traveled road. The child's perception of reality is limited to his need to exercise important functions of motility, curiosity, exploration, and gathering of experiences in the wider object world away from his mother's restrictions. This "vision" of reality is very different from that of the mother, whose concern in this situation is the child's physical safety. Both visions—that is, perceptions—the toddler's and the mother's, are completely correct, although obviously the mother's better grasp of the *total* reality must dominate the toddler's more limited capacity to perceive the entire situation. In time, the toddler's capacity will expand but limitations of the perceptual grasp of reality remains forever, albeit diminishing, hopefully, with ongoing experience.

Although it would seem preferable to think that objective experiences play the major role in acquisition of reality testing, we are proposing that the patterns or programs laid down in early life play the more decisive role in determining how reality will be perceived later on. In the process of taking over more and more of the functions of the object representations, the developing child has opportunity to come closer to experiencing the reality of the world at large. This adds another reality. There are: the reality of subjective experience; the reality as the object perceives it; consensual reality—that is, acceptance of reality as presented by the object or objects; and the reality of the wider world, which is different from the world as perceived by the primary objects. The separation-individuation process, in its progression, provides opportunities to develop a more flexibly adaptive view of the object world which nevertheless always falls short of truly objective assessment of reality. There remains always a "vision" of reality. The extent to which visions dominate behavior is a measure of the relative success or failure of the capacity of the superordinate ego to achieve ascendance. In the best of circumstances perception of reality alters "true" reality to a lesser rather than a greater degree, but reality is always distorted to some extent in favor of maintaining object connection.

As an example, the child who has been restrained from running out into the road by his mother has not learned that the road is a dangerous place for him. He has only learned that running out there has a surprising effect on the mother, an effect which the child may or may not consider undesirable depending upon the state of the relationship. If the child were to conclude that the road is dangerous and to be avoided, the conclusion would be based solely upon the mother's reaction which has now been internalized. The objective real danger would remain unperceived until some later time in life.

It was Freud's belief that objective reality testing begins with the recognition of the mother's face, as it compares with the mental image. Loewald (1980) refers to a passage in *Civilization and Its Discontents* which says: "The ego detaches itself from the external world" (Freud 1930:66–68). Loewald expands this to mean that

> the psychological constitution of ego and outer world go hand in hand. . . .
> The infant's repeated experience that something, in his original feeling a
> part of him, is not always available. This repeated experience of separateness
> leads to the development of an ego which has to organize, mediate, unify.
> (1980:5)

From this Loewald postulates that there is a "primary reality" vastly different from "reality" as a finished product that is related to the "mature" ego (p. 6).

As structure develops, and as the child takes over more and more of the functions of the protecting objects, there is greater opportunity to come closer to experiencing the actual reality of the world at large, separate and distinct from the perceptions of the object. Thus, each individual's ongoing growth-promoting, separating-individuating processes provide opportunity to develop a more flexibly adaptive view of the object world, closer to the objective state of things, but always short of true reality. This function fails to a greater or lesser degree in each individual. For example, the vision of reality of the adolescent is considerably distorted by the normal separating-individuating needs of that period of life. Therefore, certain elements of structure remain outside the capacity to perceive reality and are preserved in the form of transference readiness. For this reason alone it is useful, for precise understanding of the transference, to be able to measure the extent to which these structural elements are fixed, the extent to which the superordinate ego has been able to bring them closer to objective reality—and more important to the therapeutic situation—the extent to which the therapist's efforts to become the ally of the superordinate ego can enable "truer" reality to be approached. This, after all, is the meaning of transference interpretation and transference resolution. When the analyst or therapist appears as "real" as improved perception makes possible, the transference is resolved.

CHAPTER 6
OBJECT RELATIONS

FREUD affirms that "the relation to the external world has become the decisive factor for the ego" (1933a:75). He notes repeatedly that human development is shaped to a considerable extent by the fact of a long and total dependence, but he was not able, during his lifetime, to develop the object relations aspect of psychoanalytic theory, and therefore he did not describe the precise manner in which the primary object *constitutes* that external world for the infant.

Self and object images are built out of myriad daily affective experiences that begin on day one or before. Thrust into a vastly different environment from that which existed in utero, the infant responds by coenesthetic sensing to comforting and gratifying experiences and has to process the painful and frustrating experiences that inevitably, even under optimal conditions, constitute a part of the new environment. Unable to distinguish inside from outside, unpleasant and painful stimuli which emanate from the body as well as from the surround are thought to be projected outward. If that is so, it gives the infant psychological time to build up a preponderance of positive self and object experience that will serve later to propel it into the object world. These consist of positive, affectively tinged memory traces of a benign self merged with a benign object.

In addition to affective interaction or, we might say, as an aspect of it, maternal stimulation quickens latent ego functions, the potentials for which reside in the undifferentiated matrix. They become functions such as perception when the mothering person provides carefully titrated stimuli to be perceived. Memory is quickened by repetitive experiences that enable the child to lay down memory traces. Anticipation is quickened in interaction with memory as repetitive experiences become predictable. Motility is quickened as the infant's entire body responds to the pleasure of movement. Intentionality is quickened as the infant becomes familiar with the gestalt of the human face and begins to smile at it. The other conflict-free functions become quickened as basic needs are gratified and the child is thereby freed of anxiety about them to become involved with new ego functions—to vocalize, perhaps to engage in a primitive form of thinking, to begin to form a body image by discovering thumb, toes, genitals.

Structure builds by consolidation of single experiences into "islands" and "continents," and this involves adaptive processes in both the narrower and broader senses, especially since the stimuli are so disparate that they impinge upon different sensory organs. In the narrower sense, anticipated relief from hunger, for example, is the result of many identical experiences leading to the qualitative change of the hunger cry from an objectless wail to a strident summons. The ego functions of anticipation and memory are now operative. In the broader adaptive sense, anticipation of relief combines with another sensory perception— the auditory one—(and perhaps with a sense of time) into a higher, more integrated level of function, although still on a primitive level. In this instance the auditory experience also taps into memory traces, combining with anticipation of relief to bring about a new kind of response to both inner and outer stimuli.

Where the environment is less favorable, organization fails. The smile is delayed and the second and third organizers, in turn, fail to develop at the phase-appropriate time, indicating that a different and less socially efficient form of organization of the psyche is taking place.

While much depends upon the neonate's innate capacity to extract from the environment, the opportunity and material for extraction which the mothering person is able to offer is also decisive. The milieu in which these structures are laid down consists of the primary object who constitutes the average expectable environment to which the infant brings its unique capacity for interaction.

A well-matched mother-child pair would be:

1. A child who responds to a responsive mother.
2. A less responsive child fortunately matched with a mother who extends herself.

3. A child who can reach out to a less responsive mother, forcing her to respond.

Poorly matched pairs are:

1. A child who gets little or no response even upon reaching out.
2. A child unable to make a connection with the mothering person no matter how much she reaches out.

The mother's preparedness for the specific encounter with her infant may be said to originate in her own childhood: with reinforcement of her primary femininity by her parents' affirmation of it; with firm acquisition of gender identity in her second year of life; with lifelong knowledge of her biological destiny to bear children; with the oedipal wish to bear her father's child and the resolution of that wish, resulting in the search for a man of her own generation to father her child. Thus the life of a girl and woman includes conscious and unconscious preparation for motherhood. Her choice of a husband involves evaluation, sometimes conscious, of his potential for fatherhood. With conception and pregnancy the past preparation is brought to bear on fantasy production as the mother-to-be begins her side of the relationship with the as-yet-unknown person who will join her in a dyadic experience that will have decisive bearing upon the child's development and will promote developmental change in the mother as well (Benedek 1959).

The self and object images, merged at first, separate out gradually as the infant sorts out that which is self from that which is other. Physiology plays a part as the separating thrust, powered by the aggressive drive, initiates the long separation-individuation process. The differentiating infant matures physically to the point where molding to the mother's body is no longer possible. The child begins to view the object from a distance, thereby establishing physical as well as psychological boundaries. Semantic communication replaces earlier vocalization and verbalization and temporarily takes on a negative tinge in identification with the no-saying aggressor. From that point on, differentiation proceeds apace through the practicing and rapprochement subphases. There are normal regressions as well as progressions, but in the long pull, the child is on the way to object constancy by approximately three years of age (Mahler).

The drives do not develop in equal quantity. Libido is in the ascendancy at the beginning of life to propel the infant into the symbiotic unity. Libido begins to wane toward the end of symbiosis as the aggressive drive gains ascendancy over it, initiating the thrust into the separation-individuation process.

Within the first year of life the structuring process produces some of the prototypical patterns of organization which constitute early forms of object relations. All development involves internalization—processes whereby both positive and negative affective experiences emanating from interaction with the external world are taken in. The manner in which each experience is put to use depends upon the state of structuralization at the time the experience takes place, for it is that state which determines the capacity to process experience. We find it convenient and explanatory to use a modern metaphor to describe these structures as "programs" which are established along undifferentiated psychophysiological pathways.

The recent infant observations (Brazelton et al. 1975; Osofsky 1979; Stern 1980) suggest that there is primitive negotiation with the object shortly after birth. Brazelton's films show a three- or four-week-old infant making mouth movements similar to or identical with the mouth movements of the mother. This appears to be responsive behavior on the part of the infant, for a relatively long interval in the presence of the mother, for a shorter period of time when the father is present, and not at all in the presence of a stranger. These observations raise questions that are not easily answered.

Such activity can hardly be volitional at so early an age, nor can it be indicative of the existence of psychic structure. Neither does description of it as reflexive provide a complete enough answer to why it occurs. Because the danger of adultomorphic speculation is so great, more research will have to go into the exploration of why an infant, believed to be lacking the ability to distinguish inside from outside and also lacking internalizations and structure, nevertheless appears to respond to the external object in an imitative manner.

Traditionally, it was believed that imitation is the first of the intaking processes. These neonatal studies suggest the possibility that something like imprinting occurs immediately upon birth, much as Spitz had already suggested. But according to Mahler, there is an innate drive toward individuation. Therefore imprinting can play only a small and short-lived role for the human infant; it is superseded quite early by the infant's attempts at mastery, a reflection of the functioning of the aggressive drive.

The conclusions reached by child observationalists inevitably raises the question "There have always been infants; why wasn't this known before?" The answer is, of course, is that infants are not cared for by trained observers. Freud (1905b) notes that in his "Three Essays on the Theory of Sexuality" he had "discovered" that which every children's nurse already knew.

Also to be noted is that, before there is a frame of reference around which scientists orient their investigations, some factors escape observation. The cause of marasmus was unknown before Spitz was called in to investigate the alarming incidence of infantile deaths in a children's hospital. His background in psychoanalysis, added to his experience in infant observation, provided the framework for discovery of the solution to the vexing question of why those infants died so mysteriously in spite of the fact that they were receiving excellent physical care.

Freud comments about his 1905 essay: "If mankind had been able to learn from a direct observation of children, these three essays could have remained unwritten" (1920b:133). He was in fact commenting that evidence of infantile sexuality was there to be seen by anyone capable of perceiving the obvious. Post-Victorian taboo on sexual matters also prevented this recognition. Freud had been able to notice it because his psychoanalytic researches provided the framework into which this new data fit.

It is a fact, however, that infant observation is not in the forefront of psychoanalytic investigation. For a long time, there were only Spitz's and Mahler's studies. Their work has not enjoyed unqualified acceptance even among psychoanalysts. Kohut overlooks that the vision of a trained observer can see extraordinary features in ordinary-appearing behavior.

Now child observation is becoming a bit more fashionable among a few child analysts, as well as pediatricians and other nonanalytic observers such as child psychiatrists and psychologists. Nonanalytic interpretations of data appear to refute the conceptualizations arrived at by psychoanalytic child observation. For example, now that we are alerted to infant behavior, it is being reported that infants smile long before three months. The all-too-hasty conclusion is that Spitz is mistaken. In fact, he is mistaken only in his timetable, which does seem a bit slow, probably because his observations were carried out for the most part with institutionalized children. But the timing represents the least and most dispensable aspect of his work. Children in families where there is adequate partnering in the dyad have been observed to smile at an earlier age than three months. The error in timing does not invalidate the important conclusions about the organizers of the psyche. In fact, it shows that organization is quickened by maternal stimulation; therefore the indicators of the level of organization appear earlier.

Mahler's conclusions about a normal autistic phase are similarly challenged because it has been observed that normal neonates are not in a total dozing, vegetative, splanchnic state (Stern 1980). We, too, have some question about whether there is a normal autistic phase. But we do not think that the mere facts that the neonate stares at the mother on the first day of life, and responds to her by "imitating" her mouth movements shortly thereafter, constitute sufficient data to disprove Mahler on that point. Our question is based upon consideration of the inborn capacities of the infant. Normal infants possess apparatuses that are potentiated upon contact with the average expectable environment because the neonate is indeed at the peak of adaptive capacity. The new evidence shows only that there is alertness and reception of input earlier than was supposed.

We think of the early days and weeks of life as time spent in forming a connection with the primary object in preparation for the essential symbiotic phase. If early connection fails because of deficiency on either side of the dyad, further development then follows such a deviant course that pathological autism may well ensue; innate apparatuses are not quickened at the age-appropriate time. They remain as unrealized potential and may not be quickened belatedly because, for some functions, timing is of the essence. Therefore, while autism is clearly a pathology, it does not appear to us that it can also be a normal phase because, normally, apparatuses develop very rapidly after quickening. To our way of thinking, then, the recent information about neonatal behavior is not directly a refutation of Mahler as has been claimed. It corrects a misperception on her part that may have come about because her first studies were of psychotic children.

Spitz (1965) found that neonatal reception is in the coenesthetic mode. When the shift to diacritic perception takes place, that earlier form of processing input is not entirely superseded. Earlier forms of object seeking persist throughout life and influence behavior in subtle ways. Spitz says:

> It is difficult, if not impossible, to find a formula to express the multiform, silent ebb and flow, the mute invisible tides, powerful and at the same time subtle, which pervade these relations. It can never be sufficiently stressed, nor too often repeated, that object relations take place as a constant inter- action between two very unequal partners . . . that each provokes the re- sponses of the other; that this interpersonal relation creates a field of constantly shifting forces. (1965:211–12)

The importance of the coenesthetic mode and its influence upon all forms of later behavior has not been sufficiently exploited in theory construction. That it persists explains why early life—the unforgettable and the unrememberable—remains unconscious and is retrievable only in reflected (transferential) form. Explained also is why the many feel- ings, moods, and attitudes become rigidly fixed in some individuals and flexibly amenable to reality testing in others, depending upon the failure or success of the superordinate ego.

The new information from recent infant observation—that neonates are more alert and responsive than was hitherto thought possible—is valuable in a way that these investigators have not thought. It provides the centerpiece to a puzzle, enabling us better to fit together several concepts that have been known for some time. In retrospect these well- understood matters can now be seen to be parts of a larger whole. The new information confirms both Hartmann and Spitz and, above all, it completes the puzzle of human development, providing an organizing principle around which processes already well known may be even better understood.

Proven is

1. that the unconscious exists and is derived from the earliest experiences in life;
2. that the encounter of the normally endowed neonate with an average expectable environment is critical for development;
3. that the symbiotic experience is essential for further development, as is the thrust into the separation-individuation process;
4. that early modes of object connection are never lost and exert powerful influence upon transference phenomena.

Emphatically affirmed is the central importance of the object relations factor in human development.

As growth proceeds toward higher levels of separation and individuation, constant mental representations are formed. We use the term *representation* here following Lichtenberg (1975) to connote that structures that formerly existed as fleeting images have coalesced and acquired stability and constancy. They become more or less fixed as the result of stabilization, and the object representations may then be thought of as a "slot" containing qualities and characteristics which derive from the specific affective experiences with the primary object, now combined by the individual response into a unique creation.

Earlier in the process of theory construction it was thought that the first experiences result in the establishment of self and object representations (Jacobson). Now we find that the matter is considerably more complex. What is established are not simply mental representations but *resultants* of the interaction or negotiations between self and object at the varying degrees of differentiation that obtain in the entire course of the separation-individuation process. It is these resultants that become internalized and form structures. This is how, eventually, distinct and unique-to-each-individual patterning of self and object experience becomes the template for all future object relations. The concept of *object relations* refers to the nature and quality of this "slot" which is shaped into a specific form of readiness for future object negotiations and for the formation of object relationships.

Later in life, images of new external objects, some of whom will fit more easily and some less easily, will be fed in this slot. It contains the program developed in the early years and is the model against which all other persons are measured. In adult life, therefore, contemporary objects are subjected to reality testing, sometimes to a greater and sometimes to a lesser degree—greater if the program can be altered by reality testing in a flexible manner because of competent functioning of the superordinate ego, lesser if the patterned or programmed response is rigidly fixed. In all circumstances there is an irreducible minimum of intrusion of past object relations patterns upon current object negotiation because, even under the best of circumstances, reality testing gives way in some degree in favor of maintaining object ties.

CHAPTER 7
THE FUNCTIONS OF
THE OBJECT REPRESENTATIONS

WE ARE NOT accustomed to thinking of the object representations as having functions. Yet the very fact that the object is
needed as the essential partner in the dyadic experience within which
development takes place implies function. The obvious function of the
object is provision of the physical and psychological care without which
the neonate cannot survive. Somewhat less obvious is that the mental
images of the object, including the earliest, as they accrue, are essential
to the structuring of self and object relations.

Those images build in the medium of affectively tinged experiences,
both the gratifying and the frustrating ones. It is believed that the
infant projects negatively tinged images to the outside to maintain a
sense of pleasurable stability, a "good" self-object image upon which
to build the foundation for self-esteem. When a modicum of capacity
to test reality is quickened, it becomes possible for the infant to realize
that both gratifying and frustrating experiences emanate from interaction with the same set of object images. Where gratifying experiences
preponderate, this realization results in fusion of both kinds of images
into the representation of a single, whole, other person. Where negatively tinged experiences are overwhelming, development of the capacity
to recognize that the object images represent a single, whole, other
person is retarded at best and not at all accomplished at worst. Where
that happens futile search for good self and object images continues,
perhaps throughout life. This is another way of saying that, in good
enough circumstances, disparate self and object images coalesce into
stable representations. It says also that in many narcissistic and borderline conditions this essential developmental step cannot be taken
without therapeutic assistance.

There is a parallel process that is simultaneous with internalization—alteration in the already acquired self and object representations to encompass new experiences as they occur. These alterations are qualitative, promoted by increased autonomy and increasing competence of ego functions, particularly the function of reality testing. Normal disappointment and disillusionment can be tolerated within an organization that has integrated earlier frustrations in good enough balance with positive experience. So-called negative or frustrating experiences, in tolerable doses, force important changes in the object representations, such as diminution of belief in their omniscience and omnipotence, with greater reliance upon self-competence. Where there is good enough balance of positive and negative experience, the negative aspects become assimilated in a continuous organizing process that turns them to adaptive advantage.

Diminution of omniscience and omnipotence results from improved perception of reality. This, however, is limited by the capacity of the perceptual apparatus of the infant and young child. To a child (perhaps to all of us to a lesser degree) there is no objective reality. The complete instrument that perceives is created out of the several senses with which the human being is endowed, and includes the capacity to process the information as it registers. Even where senses such as vision, smell, hearing, touch, and the like are unimpaired, that which is being sensed has to be filtered through a mental apparatus, using past as well as present experience to create a new percept. Opportunities for distortion exist in all parts of that process.

We have referred to the several attempts to describe and define the "intaking" processes, and we have shown that the fine distinctions among introjection, incorporation, and identification are no longer so essential because they are subsumed under the concept we are introducing here—that aspects and functions of the object representations are transferred to the self representations at all levels of development. Whether the infant "introjects" while the older child "identifies" or "incorporates" becomes irrelevant in this new light. Sandler and Rosenblatt (1962) attempt to illustrate the difference between identification and introjection. They present the example of a child whose parents, leaving for the evening, admonish him not to stay up too late. If he identifies, he will stay up late, while if he introjects, he will go to bed early. The alternative view that we present obviates straining for fine distinction. The degree of structuralization determines the sophistication of the "intaking" process which in turn determines the form of behavioral reaction.

Structuralization, differentiation, and internalization are continuous processes. The young infant merges with the gratifying object-images-experienced-as-part-of-the-self-images; the separating-individuating toddler "absorbs" or transfers aspects of the object representations to the ever-differentiating self representations; the oedipal child begins to organize the precipitate of parental values (which, until the first round of resolution of the Oedipus complex, existed as superego components) into a value system of his or her own.

Thinking of development as ongoing, continuous, and ceaseless suggests that we think of all of these processes as internalizations, differing qualitatively to correlate with the increasing capacity of the individual to create ever-greater boundaries between self and object images and representations. But this very process of internalization, as we understand it, is not a simple one of becoming like the object. Internalization operates creatively. Here we have to take into account individual endowment, level of development insofar as that provides experience in ever-broader contexts of reality, and the fact that is central to our theory of object relations—namely, that what is internalized is the *resultant,* or product, of the unique manner in which each individual processes experience. Central to this process is the operation of the ego-as-a-whole, the superordinate ego.

Internalization is essential to promote ever-higher degrees of ego autonomy, which escalates as some of the functions of the object representations are taken over by the self representations.

The functions of the object representations gradually wane as autonomy increases. The child who has been soothed begins to be able to soothe himself or herself. The infant who was fed grasps the feeding spoon in an autonomous thrust. The toddler begins to insist upon dressing himself or herself. In such manner, the self representations acquire new and higher-level functions. This has already been suggested by Sandler and Rosenblatt (1962), who refer to identification as a modification of the self representation on the basis of modeling it on an object representation.

The overall function of the object representation is to provide "material" for the developing child to process. This material consists, in large measure, of the myriad daily affective interactions that contribute to building structure. Such a view, of course, merely reemphasizes the need for the object in human development. It also opens avenues for elaborating a more orderly system of psychological development.

Weiss (1960) describes a halfway or transitional position in the ongoing process of internalization, a moment in developmental time when the absent external object is experienced as a "psychic presence" before becoming more fully internalized. The object (in more modern terms, the object representation) is thought of as guiding or issuing commands, of being with the individual in an imaginary way. As internalization proceeds to ever-higher levels, this mental representation of the actual external object is no longer needed because the individual can now perform that function within himself or herself. The self representation may then be said to have absorbed the function previously performed by the object representation. That function is always altered by the unique modifications that each individual introduces to make it his or her own, given a functioning superordinate ego. This comes close to Hartmann and Loewenstein when they say, "Critical situations will reveal the threshold of integration: i.e., the degree to which the results of identification have become part of our own" (1962:52–53).

The functions of the object representations are:

1. Provision of safety feeling.
2. Establishment of internal regulatory functions.
3. Promotion of ego autonomy.
4. Serving as a model for character formation.
5. Promotion of superego development.
6. Provision of an "ego ideal."
7. Enforcing resolution of oedipal wishes, thereby enabling the child to enter latency.

1. Provision of Safety Feeling

It is now believed that the objectless state may be of shorter duration than was heretofore thought. This affirms that there is an avenue of psychological connection between infant and mothering person at the outset, and that merged self and object images come into being very early in the life of the child. The avenue of connection is reflexive at first. As more senses come into play it becomes a well-trod pathway that leads to the accrual of more definitive self and object images, at first merged and then gradually becoming differentiated.

As we observe infants attacking the tasks of physical maturation, we find clues to understanding the accompanying mental processes. Infants struggle to raise their heads, to control their limbs, to try to crawl and stand. This is where the construct mental representation is so useful in organizing observed data. It enables us to speculate that, by the very intensity of their efforts, self-images with distinct goals are forming. These infants are indeed at the peak of adaptive capacity.

Physical maturation proceeds most efficiently in a climate of safety— of a comfortable and secure harmony between the mental images of the self and the images of the object. Under such conditions the functions of the object images or representations alter and begin to diminish in importance as the self-images take these functions over. Sandler (1960) thinks that a safety feeling constitutes an integral aspect of structure. Sandler and Joffe say:

> As feelings differentiate, one type of feeling comes to play a major role in the regulation of experience; indeed to such a degree that its maintenance above a minimum level (when it falls or threatens to fall below that level) becomes the dominant criterion in determining the activity of the psychic apparatus. (1969:84)

Formation and internalization of object images provide means for coping with the periods when the external object is absent. Not only is this adaptive because the object cannot always be present, but, by change in function (Hartmann), it contributes to ego autonomy. This means that the very absence of the safety-providing external object is growth promoting if the absence does not stretch out beyond the length of time that the infant's still very shallow level of internalization can tolerate. If absence of the object exceeds the limits of the infant's capacity to retain object images, there is object loss. This is difficult to repair, and with too long an absence of the real object, anaclitic depression (Spitz) may even become irreversible. But if there is optimal but not excessive physical separation, establishment of images of the absent object enhances establishment of the self-images as well. In the midst of the frustration of the object's absence, the self-images build by establishing increasingly complex mental images of both self and object. Involved in this process, of course, are the ego functions of memory and anticipation.

The function of motility is also maturing during this developmental period as it is exercised daily with increasing motor competence. The infant becomes vulnerable to the daily disasters of life in the wider world. We call them disasters because an event such as a bump or fall, which appears insignificant to the adult, can elicit a reaction in the infant that requires the soothing presence of the maternal object. External restraint, when imposed for safety, offends the infant's omnipotence but does not usually inhibit strivings, and it reinforces safety feelings.

In optimal circumstances the child's internal sense of safety in the midst of great change derives from a comfortable equilibrium between the still-somewhat-merged self and object images and the wider object world. It is the sense of safety that permits the child to undertake tasks which must feel enormously risky, such as standing up and letting go— unclutching.

There is a psychological analogue to the physical act of unclutching. The hand grasp reflex is present at birth. As physical development proceeds, the infant's hands are seen clutching each other and pulling free. That which was a reflex begins to come under volitional control. But the control of this movement is acquired in two stages—first, the infant is able only to clutch; later, the ability to unclutch or let go is developed. By the time of the second organizer the primary object is cathected or, to put it metaphorically, clutched. At the practicing subphase, the exploration of the wider world involves a temporary unclutching. However, the presence of the object is still necessary most of the time. But, as is true of most expansion into the wider world, the toddler soon discovers that the world is not his or her oyster (Mahler). This realization and the accompanying separation anxiety propels the return to home base that is characteristic of the rapprochement subphase, which may now be redescribed as a process of reestablishing the external object at the center of safety.

As rapidly expanding physical capabilities impel the child toward the wider world, the primary object has to become strongly cathected as a mental representation in order that the safety feeling be maintained during the expansion of that world. Unclutching of the real external object is made possible by internalization, by "clutching" at a higher (more abstract) level, including within that process absorption of the safety feeling. By this means the external object can first be safely "unclutched," then, as the function of the object representation diminishes, a new level of autonomy is reached.

At the same time the process of identity formation is beginning to accelerate. The child becomes oppositional, reflecting the partially differentiated state of the self and object images. Here, under somewhat less than optimal circumstances, a host of symptoms such as feeding and other problems may appear, reflecting disharmony between the self and object images. Growth will proceed, but with conflict. Whether the conflict is between the incompletely differentiated self and object images or is intersystemic is determined by the degrees of separation and internalization.

In certain pathological adult structures there remains but a minimal sense of safety which is easily lost. The object representation, although retaining powerful access to the self representation, is preponderantly negative because it has not fulfilled the function of affirming autonomy.

A patient reported feeling greatly agitated because a friend had invited him to have lunch. To the patient this felt like a demand, which created much anxiety and distress. As the patient put it, "That's a lot of anxiety for a lousy lunch," indicating rather intact reality testing despite the anxiety.

The self representation had become overwhelmed by the fixed assumption of a strong and overpowering object representation that would not allow autonomous functioning. This had little to do with the reality of the external object in the present, and much more to do with the existence of a relatively unalterable "slot."

The therapist helped him look at the very simple alternative which had not presented itself to him. He could choose to decline the invitation. This intervention leans heavily on an intact capacity for reality testing that is temporarily overthrown when the object in reality is forced into a preestablished and rigidly fixed "slot." Calling upon the capacity for reality testing helps the patient distinguish past from present, to reestablish wavering ego autonomy, and to achieve a sharper definition of the self representation.

This illustrates how ego autonomy is impaired by a negatively cathected object image. The object is greatly needed despite negative cathexis; therefore its power is greatly exaggerated. The effect is a narcissistic imbalance. In the powerful but negative object connection, whatever modicum of safety feeling exists is obliterated. Freud knew this in a certain way. He says:

> We cannot avoid giving our attention for a moment longer to the ego's object-identifications. If they obtain the upper hand, and become too numerous, unduly powerful and incompatible with one another, a pathological outcome will not be far off. (1923:30)

In such cases the object representation has failed in the major function of enabling separation-individuation to proceed in safety, thereby failing to further autonomous functioning. This contrasts with the more normal experience in which conflict aroused by separation anxiety is more rather than less resolved.

2. Establishment of Internal Regulatory Functions

Another function of the object representation is the imposition of limits. Socialization of the infant is accomplished as regulations which had been imposed from without are assumed by the self representation. The task, for a child, is enormous. Not only must external restrictions be internalized but, assisted by reaction-formation and change in function, the child must learn to like them. This turnabout is in the service of the reestablishment of reasonably positive affective balance between the mental representations of the hitherto pleasure-seeking self-images and the prohibiting object images. Where imbalance remains, the consequence is either too much passivity or excessive rebellion.

3. *Promotion of Ego Autonomy*

The good enough, growth-promoting parent allows functions, both physical and psychological, to be taken over gradually as the capabilities of the child increase. In that way, which normally is rarely smooth or comfortable, functions that are almost within the child's grasp are turned over to him or her. This involves, on the parental side, the ability to "clutch" as well as to relinquish—to hold the child back if the child assumes functions prematurely. Spitz describes the parental role of assuring that maturation and development keep pace one with the other. There are critical periods when they *must* coincide if further development is to proceed smoothly.

There is a tendency to confuse *independence* with *ego autonomy*. Independence is most clearly represented in action, although it is not restricted to action. A child takes an independent step when he or she no longer needs to hold on while attempting to walk. The correct connotation of *autonomy* is in Hartmann's sense—the ego functions autonomously when it is not bound up in conflict. Relative autonomy is acquired through comfortable acquisition of functions of the object representations with minimal conflict.

For illustration, we may refer once again to Kris' comparison of the "Good Hour" with the "Pseudo-Good Hour." The patient is functioning autonomously in the "Good Hour" because the analysis has reached the point where functions of the analyst have been transferred to the patient. There is a dream, to which the patient associates comfortably, and the associations lead to an interpretation which the patient can easily make himself. The analysis is coming to an end as the functions of the analyst wane.

In the "Pseudo-Good Hour" the affective climate is a hostile one. The patient resents the analyst's interventions and declares himself able to go on with the hour in his own way in a premature assertion of independence that represents rebellion, not yet autonomy. The negative affect is a sign that the object relationship (transference) is still a conflictual one in which there is an imbalance of hostile over positive affect.

4. *Serving as a Model for Character Formation*

Early in his writings Freud describes character in terms of a cannibal-istic phase in which the act of devouring is the prototype of identifi-cation. By 1917 he writes about identification as a preliminary stage of object choice. By 1921 he is able to expand the concept of identi-fication by enumerating three forms: the original one of emotional tie to an object before object cathexis; a regressive substitute for a lost libidinal object tie; and as arising out of a new perception of a common quality shared with another person. In this third description of iden-tification Freud begins to think of identification as a normal process of development. By 1923 he becomes much clearer about that process. He refers there to replacement of an object cathexis by identification, adding;

> At that time [1917], however, we did not appreciate the full significance
> of this process and did not know how common and typical it is. Since then
> we have come to understand that this kind of substitution has a great share
> in determining the form taken by the ego and that it makes an essential
> contribution toward building up what is called its character. (p. 28)

Jacobson frees the earlier concept of identification from its sole func-tion as defense by introducing the concept of selective identification. No longer is it merely the result of abandoned object cathexes. It becomes a growth-promoting avenue for expansion of the object world, while leaving room for retention of the safety of object connection. As movement away from the real external object proceeds, the object rep-resentation serves as stimulus for that movement, as well as guide and moderator of the pace, to ensure that the developing child does not exceed his or her capacity to endure the physical and psychological distance.

The object representation as a model diminishes in usefulness as autonomous capacities take over. The model has to be "unclutched." In this process, severing the connection is accomplished without object loss because the selected aspects of the object representation are inter-nalized to become part of the self representation.

5. *Promotion of Superego Development*

At no other point in development are processes of internalization and the transfer of function from object representation to self representation as vital to development as in superego formation.

Superego formation (chapter 2) is a long process which begins with the establishment of superego components (Hartmann & Loewenstein 1962). These are internalized "islands" of parental prohibitions, demands, and values. With development, the components coalesce into a discrete structure around the time of the waning of the Oedipus complex. Jacobson refers to superego formation as

> a slow process. It begins with the acceptance of "sphincter morality." But only at the end of the oedipal phase have the building up, the integration, and organization of superego identifications proceeded far enough to create firm moral codes. Centered about the incest taboo and the law against patricide, they begin at this stage to become independent of the parents and to displace the conflicts . . . onto the inner, mental stage. (1964:119)

Positive, affectionately tinged identifications with both parents play crucial roles in the process of superego formation. Although it is still believed that the superego as a discrete agency, formed from its components, is the "heir" to the Oedipus complex, the timetable has altered since the earlier view that resolution is accomplished in the childhood period. Jacobson thinks that it extends to adolescence. We (1968) regard oedipal resolution, and therefore superego formation, as a process that continues in several rounds through the life cycle.

This introduces the thought that not only is there room for transfer of functions of *primary* object representations to the self representation, but that objects encountered later in life play a role in the developmental process. It is in that light that we (1968) consider marriage and parenthood to be developmental phases.

6. *Provision of an "Ego Ideal"*

Moore and Fine define the ego ideal as

> the images of the *self* to which the individual aspires consciously and un-

consciously, and against which he measures himself. It is based on identification with the parents and other early environmental figures, as they actually are, were in the past, or as they have been idealized. (1967:93)

Jacobson writes of transforming the "primitive, wishful images of the self and love objects into a unified ego ideal" (1964:93). While we employ the familiar term *ego ideal,* we do not think it useful to ascribe specific differentiated functions to ego ideal, superego, or ego. That certain qualities of the object are internalized to become characterological features of the self is beyond question. By its very definition the concept of the ego ideal includes transfer of function. The function here is not something concrete that the object *performs* but rather an abstract aspect of character, something that the object *is* or is perceived to be. Thus provision of an ego ideal is closely related to character formation.

7. *Enforcing Resolution of Oedipal Wishes, Thereby Enabling the Child To Enter Latency*

Reality testing forces the oedipal child to perceive that he or she is not equipped, either biologically or psychologically, to fulfill an adult role. Incestuous wishes at the first round of the oedipal conflict are the consequence, not of adult capacity to love and to perform sexually, but of having reached a new level of development which involves the genital apparatus for the first time in object-directed, as contrasted with auto-erotic purposes.

Identification intensifies at this level—the boy with the father and the girl with the mother—as a mechanism for overcoming the rivalry. Transferred from the object representations to the self representation here are attitudes of opposition to the rivalrous feelings. Safety feelings are maintained by means of repression of sexual wishes. This leads first to entry into latency and contributes, later in life, to the ability to seek out new, nonincestuous objects.

CHAPTER 8
MODES OF TRANSFERENCE

BEGINNING with Freud's recognition that transference constitutes a key element of the psychoanalytic treatment process, the
use of transference has been painstakingly described in the literature.
There are controversies about what it is and how it is to be used
(Friedman 1984; Gill 1954, 1984). Until fairly recently, its use in
psychotherapy was severely limited. Some twenty or more years ago,
psychiatrists believed that the development of a transference in psychotherapy was undesirable and means to avoid it were devised. When
transferences inevitably developed, the technique for dealing with them
was to "dilute" them by diverting the patient's interest to objects
outside the therapeutic situation. With burgeoning knowledge about
understructured personalities and with the realization that, welcome or
not, transferences form, that technical assumption has been revised.

Transference is defined as

> the displacement of patterns of feeling and behavior, originally experienced
> with significant figures of one's childhood, to individuals in current rela-
> tionships. This unconscious process thus brings about a repetition, not con-
> sciously perceived, of attitudes, fantasies and emotions of love, hate, anger
> etc., under many different circumstances (Moore & Fine 1967:89).

This definition emphasizes the unconscious quality, the repetition,
the displacement, and the affective nature of transference phenomena.
More pertinent to our present purpose is Freud's 1905 definition. He
refers to transference as a "special class of mental *structures* . . . new
editions or facsimiles [which] . . . replace some earlier person"
(1905a:116, italics ours).

Both these definitions contain the following component elements:

1. Transference involves structures—that is, patterned forms of organization of memory, affect, and behavior.
2. The existence of such structures indicates that the early experiences which have produced them in their unique and specific forms persist throughout life, influencing the forms of object relations and thus the modes of transference.
3. It is the persistence of such structures that is responsible for displacement from an affective memory of the past onto a real object in the present. This is, in fact, a failure in reality testing, a distortion of reality. There is confusion not only between past and present but also between the object representations and real, external persons.

We distinguish between the transferences of the structured personalities and those of the understructured because of the differences in degrees of structuralization and internalization, which make for qualitative differences in the manner or modes of transference. This way of thinking is reflected in the diagnostic considerations in the Fulcrum of Development (1979:64–86).

But the matter is not simple. While all structured personalities share the tendency to transfer from whole object representations of the past, the capacity to do so varies from one understructured personality to another because, until self and object constancy are reached, levels of object relations differ from one individual to another and even fluctuate from time to time in the same individual. Therefore, it is not possible to say about all understructured personalities that they elaborate transferences that are similar in quality, as we are able to say about the structured personalities.

The mode of transference is a factor of the level of development. Levels range from experiencing the therapist (and all other persons) as part of the self representations at varying degrees of self-object differentiation. The therapist may be someone with whom to repeat experiences with the primary object because such experience was overgratifying, or the opposite, because there was deprivation to be compensated for. Or the "transference" may be dominated by the wish to retain the negatively cathected object for fear of object loss. These modes of transference deviate considerably from that of the person who, having attained self and object constancy, experiences self and others as separate, whole persons. Only when self and object constancy obtains can feelings, attitudes, and behavior first experienced with a primary object be *transferred* to the object in the present.

Although structuralization and internalization proceed in a more rather than less interrelated manner, they do not necessarily maintain an even pace. The understructured personalities who are functioning with higher degrees of internalization elaborate transferences which differ only slightly from the transferences of the structured personalities. Those with less structure, less internalization, and a lesser level of self and object relations tend more to relate to the analyst or therapist (and to all other persons, for that matter) as though that other were, in some degree, part of the self.

For a while we were reluctant to designate the distortions in object relations of the understructured personalities as they appear in the therapeutic situation as *transference*. That position had the advantage of preserving the concept of transference in its original form and consigning to another category of the therapeutic relationship the behavior of the understructured patient toward the analyst or therapist. We were persuaded (principally by Fleming, in a personal communication) to forgo this precision for the sake of adhering to the vocabulary of the majority of analysts and therapists. The distinction we arrived at then was between interpretable and uninterpretable transference. Our intent was to imply that in the "transferences" of the understructured personalities not very much is transferred. Rather, such patients seek to replicate early object experience or to fulfill early object need. This, it will be recognized, is not very different from the distinction Freud made between the narcissistic neuroses and the transference neuroses.

Psychoanalytic technique was elaborated for the purpose of uncovering repressed memories—that is, for finding what *was*. Excavation of what *was* remains the goal in the treatment of the structured (neurotic) as well as in the treatment of certain types of understructured patients. The understructured patient who was overindulged presents an attitude of entitlement, palpable in the transference, reflecting expectation of indulgence. There *was,* one might say, too much. These understructured personalities are seeking to replicate early object experience by attempting to fit the therapist into the predetermined "slot" of an omnipotent part of the self that never says no to itself.

The patient who is seeking fulfillment of early object need also longs for gratification, but is unable to define that need. It exists in the form of something vague that is missing. These patients are engaged in a search for what *was not*. In a most interesting contribution to the much-disputed concept of penis envy, Grossman and Stewart (1976) suggest that a believed-to-be missing penis is something concrete that the girl can use as a metaphor to represent vague dissatisfactions that cannot be verbalized specifically. In a certain sense, the girl who feels that something is missing has an "advantage" in finding a means to express that, while the boy may be left with a longing that he cannot communicate. The interpretation that he feels castrated only compounds the problem because he can then reassure himself with the reality that his penis is not missing. But what happens to the persistent feeling that something is indeed missing!

With understructured patients who have had inadequate subphase experience and are therefore overdeprived, the therapeutic search is not only for what *was not,* but for what solution (usually in narcissistic form) the individual has created.

No adult hurt by childhood deprivation arrives in the consultation room with open "wounds" for the therapist to heal. The protective scab that has formed consists of a narcissistic solution which was adaptive at the time of formation (Blanck & Blanck 1979). By that we mean that the missing part of the self is acquired by joining whatever lies at hand. The most common of such solutions is union with the affect of the object—a depressed mother, for example. The child unites with the affect in an attempt to extract what is available from the inadequate environment. Other solutions involve attachment to reliable inanimate objects such as the transitional object, which becomes permanent rather than transitional and thus acquires the status of a fetish. Still other solutions involve creation of a fantasy object. An example of that is an imaginary companion, or a fairy godmother. Again, as with the transitional object, these may be normal temporary fantasies in childhood which become pathological when they become permanent. Narcissistic solutions are contrived at whichever developmental level the needed partner in the dyad failed in her function.

Obviously, to seek out that which was missing is inherently more difficult than to rediscover that which once existed. This is not to say that the therapist is required to gratify, even when the precise nature of the need becomes known. But detecting it is no easy matter. The search is for which quality and quantity of absence of phase-appropriate, self-object affective experience in early, usually preverbal life has left what kind of void. And because of the "scab" the patient is relatively unavailable for new object connection. Those who are altogether defended in that way probably do not seek treatment. The person who arrives at the consultation room does so because the childhood attempt at adaptation has become maladaptive—the adaptation in the form of a narcissistic solution impairs contemporary relationships. Always, the relative imperviousness of the scab is an important factor in the prognosis. In a certain sense Freud is correct when he says that the narcissistic neuroses are untreatable (1914b). Modern theory and technique provide a more favorable prognosis. Probably those narcissistic persons who are content with the "arrangement" do not present themselves for treatment. Those who do seek treatment arrive with a scab, it is true. But the therapist who is not overzealous can wait until the scab falls off. To leave the metaphor, the therapist remains available, holding out opportunity for connection, waiting for the patient to provide the avenue for entrée. As for prognosis, treatability is a factor of the permeability of the narcissistic solution (1979).

We turn now to another aspect of the use of the transference—assessment of the level of object relations. This is where major errors in treatment can be made.

Even if it were humanly possible, we doubt that it would be desirable that the analyst or therapist make no errors. Such perfection would reinforce the wish for an omnipotent object, thereby failing to provide incentive for the patient to enter the real object world. It does no harm to the treatment, and at any rate is unavoidable, that the therapist's "normal" personality impinges on the treatment; this includes the therapist's fallibility. Some errors inevitably occur in any treatment and can be used to advantage if the therapist or analyst is honest about them and does not become defensive. By and large, acknowledgment of error is best made by the interpretation of its effect. Agreement that one is mistaken is made sometimes, apology less often, and confession of countertransference never.

It is essential that the therapist be at the level of self and object constancy. In the past more than now one heard that it is useful in the treatment of severe pathology for the therapist to be "a little crazy." This is an alluring fallacy because it contains a grain of truth. A "crazy" therapist is better equipped to communicate in the primary process. But who will lead the patient out of that cohabited wilderness?

An equally cogent reason why the therapist's level of object relations must be at the level of self and object constancy is that it constitutes an assurance of the absolute reliability that is essential in the practice of psychotherapy and psychoanalysis. Where the therapist experiences self and others as whole persons, the need to use the patient to become part of oneself—that is, for narcissistic gratification—is obviated. The fact of the therapist's wholeness cuts down enormously on undesirable countertransference and leaves the field free for the use of countertransference in productive ways. The therapist's level of object relations, however, can usually only be repaired by the therapist's analysis.

By now it is clear that many questions arise about differences between the more highly developed structures and the less developed or understructured. These questions apply especially to diagnosis of the level of object relations which affects expectations about the patient's behavior in the transference. We (1979) elaborate on a much-overlooked observation Jacobson makes. She says: "In adult patients we must not confuse transference processes based upon displacement from one object image to another, such as from the mother onto the analyst, with projections" (1964:47).

More than is realized, the more serious errors in treatment follow from dealing with the patient on levels that are either too high or too low. These errors lie in two directions: application of classical psychoanalytic procedures on the assumption that the patient has reached self and object constancy when that is not so; and the reverse, infantilization of the patient who has reached self and object constancy by dealing with regressed levels as fixation instead of as defense.

An example of an error in diagnosing too high is that of a patient who has, let us imagine, lacked adequate subphase response. He or she reports accomplishments. The analyst follows correct analytic procedure, employing the abstinence rule which would be correct for a better-structured patient. If the patient's demand for a response becomes so insistent that the treatment is stalemated, the analyst may think about why there is such excessive demand for gratification, probably of rival-rous or exhibitionistic wishes. This resembles a resistance from the id, and may indeed be exactly that. On the other hand, if diagnosis has taken the level of object relations into account, what may be in order is to understand, not fulfill, subphase need. Interpretation of resistance or of competitive and exhibitionistic wishes in the transference would be incorrect. What we wish to make clear is that there is no therapeutic value, and much potential harm, in traditional psychoanalytic transfer-ence interpretation to an understructured patient. "You want me to admire you" may sound reasonable at first glance because it addresses the phallic level. It is wholly inaccurate at second glance because the need originated (and persists in the therapeutic situation) at a time in life when there was neither self nor other but only a merger of the two in some degree.

An example of diagnosing too low is the patient who presents herself or himself as in agonizing need for comfort, for approval, for the ther-apist's presence, for love. This may represent regression to the safety of union with the preoedipal mother as a defense against the anxiety of oedipal wishes. Such a patient will have reached self and object constancy despite the regression. If therapeutic address is to the re-gressed level, the patient will be infantilized rather than required to deal with conflict.

These variations are what make both diagnosis and correct thera-peutic intervention so difficult. The degree of merger may reflect fix-ation at or regression to a point in the separation-individuation process, greatly complicated by the fact that almost no understructured patient presents himself or herself always at the same level of object relations, whereas the structured patient with self and object constancy hardly ever regresses to the point of unawareness that the analyst or therapist is a separate, whole, other person.

The question persists: Are we still talking about transference? The answer is yes if the definition of transference is extended to refer to the entirety of the therapeutic encounter. Reluctantly, we go along part of the way with this watering down of the concept of transference for that which we hope will be the greater gain—communication with the therapeutic community. But we do not yield on the fact that there is a marked difference between the more structured and the less structured personalities in modes of transference because of factors in early object experience that influence the quality of object relations.

We have proposed that object relations arise neither out of self-images nor object images taken alone. Rather, they are formed out of the affective experiences of the self with the object, becoming the internalized *resultants* of the interaction. Thus they are unique to each individual. "Programs" of object readiness are established in early experience requiring adaptation, later in life, to the fact that real, contemporary, external objects do not fit precisely into the "slots" that have been established.

In describing modes of transference we are concerning ourselves with the origin of transference potential in:

1. The generally understood transference manifestations that are interpretable because self and object constancy are well established and are not regressively lost in the course of analysis.
2. The patient's fixed assumptions from early, preverbal experience that have become an unalterable aspect of character.
3. Those assumptions which, although also fixed, can yield, albeit ever so slowly, to a new and different experience of the object world—the therapeutic differential as described by Loewald (1980).

In the last two instances the object images are experienced, in varying degrees, as part of the self-images. Jacobson, in discussing primary narcissism and primary masochism, asks, "What precisely is the meaning of narcissism and masochism in the primitive psychic organization prior to the child's discovery of his own self and of the object world?" (1964:7). The same question may be raised about transference potential in the sense that the capacity to engage in transference is usually assumed to involve the capacity to engage in object relationships with separate, whole, other persons. To paraphrase Jacobson, then, what can be the meaning of object relations and therefore of transference potential in the primitive psychic organization?

Beyond noting that differences in the three modes of transference potential have their origins in different degrees of completion of the separation-individuation process, it is not yet clear what specific vicissitudes of that process determine why and how differentiation develops in some instances, while in others the self and object representations remain less than differentiated in varying degrees. It is worthwhile to attempt to determine what factors might be identified as contributing to the alteration in structure from less differentiated to more differentiated.

Probably the three broad categories into which we have cast this issue are best illustrated clinically.

Mr. A. is a young professional who is quite effective in many areas of his life. He describes an incident in which his fiancée tells him of plans for the weekend. They were to visit friends, a married couple, so that "Jane and I can bake pies for Christmas while you and John watch the football game." He is puzzled by the feelings that came over him upon hearing this. They would have been appropriate had she *commanded* him to obey. He did obey, but with poorly concealed resentment. At the end of the day he quarreled openly with his fiancée, who, on her part, objected to his obstreperous behavior.

He behaves similarly in the transference when he is asked to associate to the situation after having described it. He feels that he is being ordered, but he is able to discuss these reactions calmly after the storms, showing great surprise with himself.

This is obviously a most favorable diagnostic and prognostic sign, indicating as it does that there is a competent observing ego in the traditional sense. He does not turn the anger against himself, but is able to observe his behavior and to deal with it without excessive self-reproach and without concomitant erosion of self-esteem. Although he is surprised, he is not destroyed. Also, with analytic help, he can connect his behavior with the past when there were continuous battles with his mother over his rebellious and insubordinate behavior. He does not expect a magical cure to result from such beginning insight, but has a sober appreciation of the task ahead in working through the conflicts of the past as they remain alive in the present.

The absence of magical expectation, the very limited turning against the self, the recognition of the nature of his struggle for autonomy, are reflections of the well-functioning superordinate ego that makes it possible for him to struggle with the programs that were organized in the past and to reorganize them in the psychoanalytic process.

This case depicts the familiar, well-structured, analyzable patient, capable of elaborating a transference neurosis. What we have added is that the superordinate ego oversees functions traditionally thought to be functions of the ego of structure—such as self-observation.

Mr. B. is in his middle fifties. He had been in treatment before, with many different therapists. He is a reasonably effective middle-range executive in a corporation where he has worked for over five years. After a merger, a new set of officers took over, and although the chief executive officer had expressed great satisfaction with Mr. B's work, he dismissed him a year after the merger.

Mr. B. remained out of work for over a year, exhausted his benefits, reduced his therapy sessions because of financial pressure, and became depressed. Ultimately, he found another job, once again as a middle manager in a small corporation. Despite severe anxiety he made a very good impression because he is extremely competent in his field. The beginning salary in his new position was only slightly less than before, with a definite promise of quick advancement if he were to perform well.

The initial relief that he felt in finally finding a job consonant with his experience and which solved his growing financial emergency lasted about two weeks. Not only did his depressed state return, he also began, unconsciously, to sabotage his position. He resented the fact that he could not go home at four-thirty; every work assignment was perceived as demanding too much. This in spite of the fact that, at his level, corporate officers do not have regular hours, and he had not had them in his former position. Out of long experience with him, the analyst was soon able to discern that he was "digging in his heels," a phrase which Mr. B. had used many times before to describe his oppositional pattern of functioning.

In the benign climate of a long therapeutic relationship, Mr. B. could not only recognize the hitherto unconscious resentment, but could also find words to express his disappointment in finding himself in work that he considered beneath him. The fact that it was in his field and the reality that this new position offered far greater scope and opportunity was forgotten. The former position was nostalgically remembered in an idealized way. With recognition and verbalization of his behavior, he was able also to recall that he had felt the same way in the beginning months on the previous job. Out of these associations a fantasy emerged, roughly analogous to the family romance, in which he felt somehow that he had been deposed from his rightful kingdom.

Mr. B. was happy with this therapeutic work and felt considerably relieved, especially since he could see very clearly how he had been putting his worst foot forward in his work situation. The awareness of his behavior seemed to promise that he might work on the unconscious determinants, but that did not happen. Instead, the problem became displaced to other situations.

Mr. B.'s history of repeated job loss and termination of social relationships, with concomitant depression and immobility, came into focus and fell into a new frame of reference. There was the strong probability that reasons for the many terminations with different therapists over the course of many years might have been presented in rationalized form—that the real causes lay in his tendency to terminate relationships, not in external factors. Diagnostic thought began to revolve around the fact that, while he obviously profits from his therapy in the day-to-day experiences, he does not succeed in reorganizing some fundamental programs which continue to run off.

We (1979) referred to the capacity for reorganization as a fundamental diagnostic consideration. We believe, now, that we can identify this factor more clearly. In the case of Mr. B., the superordinate ego was not competent to overcome the fundamental fear of loss of identity in a surrender of autonomy, and so he fights for his life (identity) by using mechanisms such as withdrawal, close to catatonic immobility, and global withholding. A major symptom, impotence without physical cause, fits this diagnostic thought.

Therefore, although Mr. B. is responsive in treatment, his use of the therapeutic medium does not extend to that area where the superordinate ego is needed to take charge. He continues to require the actual presence of the therapist who performs the function of organization for him. It is in that specific sense that he cannot function autonomously. The "digging in" may be regarded as cessation of functioning. Where the superordinate ego is so deficient, insight and working through of unconscious determinants of behavior which resembles acting out are not realistic therapeutic goals.

The last case that we shall discuss illustrates that a poorly functioning superordinate ego can be helped toward better capacity in the course of treatment.

> Mrs. C. greatly fears success, but this appears to be more on the level of fear of annihilation than on the oedipal level. The fear overwhelms her functional capacities. She has extraordinary talents, but becomes terrified of her skills and usually manages to leave tasks incomplete or to finish them in a crunch, providing reinforcement for her determination to avoid all future tasks. Her avoidance of function has the distinct purpose of evading anticipated disaster.
>
> It required lengthy therapeutic work combined with ongoing diagnostic assessment for the therapist to be assured that her inability to function was not the more usual reflection of oedipal anxiety and guilt. Her almost ineradicable fantasy is that, as she is helped to function, which is what she consciously wants, the therapist takes her another step toward annihilation. This is a fixed assumption, a belief that has not yet been brought into conformity with the reality of her current experiences.
>
> Her response to the usual analytic interventions is intense rage caused by severe separation anxiety. The therapist chose to reduce the anxiety of too sharp a separation by becoming interested in the minute details of her life. This was a transitional phase of the treatment in which Mrs. C. became assured of connection and was able to begin to venture to sever it by the exercise of function at her own instead of the therapist's pace.

The following provides some dialogue around an issue brought about by Mrs. C.'s conflict around functioning. She is an accomplished musician who has studied with teachers who may be thought of as kingmakers in that they have participated in the training of first-rank concert artists. Such teachers choose their pupils very carefully, so it is clear that Mrs. C. is unusually talented. The content of the sessions over a few weeks' time is around a recital at which she has agreed to play and for which she is now preparing. She regresses to threats familiar to the therapist from the past—to call off the concert, fire the music coach, terminate therapy, and kill herself. She is afraid that she will lose the ability to read the notes, or she will lose her place, or she will be unable to play at all, or she will faint or fall off the bench. These represent fear of imminent disintegration.

PATIENT: When I feel that way it is as though I have lost myself. Part of me is looking at the other part which is paralyzed.

(Depersonalization is obvious.)

THERAPIST: Actually paralyzed?

PATIENT: No, in anticipation. During the recital I manage to keep going. But it is such agony that I never want to let it happen again.

THERAPIST: And is that when you resolve never to let yourself play again?

PATIENT: Yes.

The next session begins with a ten-minute silence.

PATIENT: I did not want to come today. Although I felt better yesterday, I became furious with you after I left. I fulminated for several hours until I realized that I want to get out of performing and that you are not letting me quit.

Now Mrs. C. has developed some capacity for realistic self-observation, contrasted with depersonalization. This was achieved by the expansion of function of the superordinate ego in the course of therapy. When she feared that the therapist was forcing her toward more separation than she could tolerate, she feared annihiliation and expressed it in the form of rage, a failure of affect differentiation (1979). At this stage of the treatment she has a better sense of intactness. But, as is evident in the dialogue, there is movement forward and back.

Now she begins to recognize that the idea of being forced is a projection. She has been helped to become aware that she had chosen to participate in the recital without having discussed it in her sessions. By this time the fixed assumption, characterological and projected, has become weakened by her recognition of the therapeutic differential (Loewald). She begins to appreciate that the therapist protects her autonomy and works with her toward her own goals.

Now she can begin to view the therapist more as a true transference object and less as an object for replication of early object need. Her mother had not been encouraging, despite her talent. This is an example of what *was not*—the object was not interested in her attraction to the piano. She longs for the therapist's interest, but fears it as a threat to her identity because she can only believe that interest would be at the level of object need where self and object images are merged.

THERAPIST: How do I stop you from quitting?

PATIENT: Oh, let's not go through that charade again. I know now that you do not stop me from quitting, but it feels as though you do and so therefore you do.

THERAPIST: This must give me a very strange role in your life.

The purpose of this intervention is to give recognition to both regressive and progressive movements within the session. At first the object representation is in a somewhat more separated position than heretofore; then, within the same sentence, it moves into a merged position: "It feels as though you do and so therefore you do." The design is to give the superordinate ego the task of "thinking" about these contradictory representations in order to become proficient in reconciling them. It may be thought of as a straddle between the merged self and object representations and the separated ones. Presenting her with this task exercises function.

To put this another way, it designates the position of her object relations, and especially that there is movement forward and back. This may be thought of as allowing the object representation to "float," now thrusting forward, now to a more regressed level. The forward thrusts, it is hoped, will gradually bring the level of object relations above where it was before treatment. To have said, "But you know by now that I do not stop you," would have been an external confrontation which would not have served to alter structure.

PATIENT: Yes. Sometimes I know that it was I who arranged the recital, so I must want to play and give recitals. But when it comes close to the time, I forget all that and see you as the one forcing me to do it even though I know better.

Here we see the vacillation between the realistic assessment of external reality because separateness is approached, and the almost instantaneous regression to the more merged state of union with the wished-for object who forces her. She is not dealing with past object representations projected onto the therapist. The primary objects (nurse and mother) were supremely indifferent. The wish for an object who forces her represents not an internalized object representation, but a wish for a real object. Object relations remain in the interpersonal realm. It becomes a task of the treatment to promote internalization.

Also illustrated are intervention where transference is not interpretable, and how the superordinate ego can be helped to function where the capacity to extract from the therapist can be quickened.

In summary, whether transference can be interpreted depends upon the basic level of object relations achieved, as well as upon the level which is operative at the moment. The capacity to utilize interpretable transference is the consequence of successful negotation of the Fulcrum of Development. It is especially important that there be intrapsychic rather than interpersonal object relations, secondary process thought, use of speech for semantic communication, and self and object constancy.

We distinguish displacement from projection. Displacement involves a *processed and structured* level of object relations, transferring to separate object B attitudes and feelings appropriate to separate object A. Projection, on the other hand, is not specifically object related. It makes use of the other person, or even merely the thought of another, for emplacement of the subject's own feelings and thoughts. Reality testing, while inaccurate in both instances, is vastly more deficient where projection is used.

CHAPTER 9
THE CONCEPT OF
THE SELF

THERE HAS BEEN ambiguity about the definition of *self* and even about the very concept throughout the history of theory construction. Freud used the German word *Ich* sometimes to refer to the self and sometimes to the ego. In an attempt to provide consistency, Strachey, in the *Standard Edition,* translated *Ich* as *ego* in every instance. This has been criticized, especially by some German-speaking analysts; obviously, Freud did sometimes mean *self*. Throughout his writings, where Freud is ambiguous, retrospective study usually reveals that it is because he has not yet clarified his thoughts on a given matter. Not until 1923, in *The Ego and the Id,* was Freud able to provide a precise definition of *ego,* finally resolving the ambiguity of his earlier usage of the term. Major psychoanalytic thinking, such as Anna Freud's work on the defensive function of the ego, was spurred by this definition.

It is taking considerably longer for *self* to be defined within the context of mainstream psychoanalytic thought, quite appropriately, since the "self" is but another construct, useful heuristically, but essentially difficult if not impossible to define with any degree of accuracy. Adler, Jung, Horney, and Sullivan all employ a concept of a self, as does Kohut (1971, 1977), but each ascribes a different meaning to it. Erikson (1959) refers to *ego identity* in an attempt to broaden the scope of psychoanalytic understanding to encompass the total person rather than drives taken alone or ego taken alone. This parallels the new philosophy that began to permeate medical thought at about the same time (Hinsie, *The Person in the Body,* 1945). The person is regarded as an integrated entity instead of a conglomeration of organs.

Although it is more than twenty years since Jacobson wrote the following statement, it remains accurate:

In recent years, psychoanalysts have paid increasing attention to the fascinating problem of identity. Of course, a fruitful discussion of this problem presupposes precise definitions of such terms as *self, ego,* and *identity* or *ego identity,* which are indispensable for constructive analytic approaches to this and many related questions. Whereas Hartmann (1950) introduced and carefully defined the distinction between the concepts of ego, self, and self representations, there exists no such generally accepted psychoanalytic definition of the concept of identity. In fact, the authors who have lately explored this subject attach quite different meanings to these terms and consequently arrive at seemingly different conclusions. (1964:xi)

Jacobson's own definition refers to "the whole person . . . including his body and body parts as well as his psychic organization and its parts" (p. 6). She adds, however, that the self is "an auxiliary descriptive term, which points to the person as a subject in distinction from the surrounding world of objects" (*ibid.*).

The self as a construct remains abstract, useful in distinguishing it from the object world. No description of the component elements can suffice; when an individual thinks of himself or herself, such thought cannot begin to encompass the totality of that which is called the self.

The ego psychologists (Hartmann, Kris, and Loewenstein) who became so productive in the late 1940s devoted themselves to consideration of the content and qualities of the individual components which make up psychic structure, the very "stuff" of ego and superego. Hartmann's work, rather than simplying theory, appears to make matters more complex by adding considerations of intrapsychic processes and conflicts to the better-understood intersystemic activities. But this apparent complexity merely follows Hartmann's observation that there are both broad and narrow aspects of adaptation, and extends it to considerations of the content of the components of the ego. It also reflects a more accurate assessment of the infinite variables of psychic structure.

Our own attempt initially was to delineate and utilize data relevant to specific functions of the individual ego components, and to combine them in a single frame of reference. We organized a chart of ego development in 1968, and an improved, more comprehensive version in 1974. Assessment of ego structure is still useful in formulating descriptive developmental diagnosis. But by 1979 we found that the most recent information about processes of development could not be encompassed in the simple device of a chart. The total person could not be understood by addressing ego, superego, and drives, important as these are. Unable to compress understanding of the whole person in a single diagnostic chart, we devised a Fulcrum of Development to show that there is a pivotal point around which structuralization, as it proceeds, alters qualitatively. This despite the fact that, with successful negotiation of the Fulcrum, psychic life shifts from interpersonal to intrapsychic; that the pathology of the understructured personality can be understood as stemming from unsuccessful negotiation of the Fulcrum; and that the pathology (neurosis) of the structured personality is the consequence of a compromise solution of intersystemic conflict.

We began also to regard pathology in terms of the person-as-a-whole. We suggested that the ego *is* the overall organizing process. Instead of defining it by its functions (Hartmann), we proposed that it be defined by its function*ing*—that is, we now focus attention upon the total person who functions, rather than upon the separate functions. This also extends the concept of adaptation to encompass the idea that there can be adaptive purpose to maladaptive behavior. Defenses serve adaptive purposes when they are first organized, only to become maladaptive later.

It also necessitates reconsideration of the concept of developmental arrest. Simple cessation of development is hardly possible in a scheme that regards development as ceaseless. In the ongoing developmental sweep, then, deficiencies become organized; they may become usefully reorganized or may persist as malformations in organization. The organization of the whole encompasses more than the sum of the parts, even those specific parts which have failed to develop to their full capacity. The following is an example:

> A patient was in treatment for several years about another matter before he was able to reveal that he has a problem with dirt that extends to irrational phobic proportions. There is nothing in his functioning to suggest this. The only clue is that this usually well-spoken, well-educated person lapses, occasionally, into neologisms. The therapy, which had focused around the presenting problem of guilt and depression at the death of his wife, seemed to be proceeding

quite well. He became able to resume his professional work and to be a reasonably competent father to his motherless children.

It is possible that the "symptom" had become exacerbated in the course of treatment—that is, that the improved level of functioning was achieved at the expense of having to mobilize such desperate defense against decompensation. On the other hand, it might have been prominent all along and could only be revealed when growing trust in the therapist made disclosure possible.

In either case, it represents a serious structural flaw. Clinicians have long been familiar with the qualitative and structural difference between compulsive cleanliness, on the one hand, and defense against decompensation, on the other.

We are obliged to think about why, in forty-odd years, this problem had not impaired functioning to a disabling degree. It did impair object relationships because of the desperate insistence that the family maintain an impossible degree of cleanliness. The therapist was unable to ascertain from the patient exactly when the symptom first appeared. Very likely it slipped in slow and indiscernible steps from ordinary hygienic precautions to phobic proportions. Also, the patient's subjective report is the only one available; it fails to distinguish normal from pathological cleanliness.

It appears that he had been able to keep this problem under better control while he was coping with the real problem of his wife's long illness with cancer. One may even speculate that the hygienic atmosphere of the sickroom contributed a final determinant to the phobia. This is reasonable because it suggests that it became a maladaptive attempt to maintain object connection with the deceased wife. What is clear is that, while he had been able to cope reasonably well with the enormous reality of a sick and dying wife, the delicate balance of structuralization was overthrown by the object loss. To express this in terms of the Fulcrum, one would think that it had been barely tilted in the direction of structuralization and therefore of more competent functioning, and that then this precarious balance tilted in the direction of the pathology that had always been a part of the total structure. Whatever defensive capacity still remains has to be employed in the service of providing a barrier to total deterioration of the personality.

In this process the capacity for symbolization loses its purpose. Whatever dirt represents in the unconscious (usually feces, sex, and hostility in the better-structured compulsive neurotic) becomes detached from its symbolic purpose in this understructured personality, and is now used as a desperate defensive measure. Sometimes this does succeed in preventing further decompensation.

The diagnosis of the "self" of this patient would have been considerably different at various times in his life; certainly the neologisms would have seemed charming in social situations. Only a therapist would be able to discern the deficits in structure suggestive of a thought disorder.

But the main thrust of this discussion is that the total person is too complex to be seen in all facets, even by the astute clinical eye. In this position, we support the current efforts to develop better understanding of the functioning of the whole person. We are convinced, however, that this is best done in an approach which takes into account the necessity to understand the way in which component parts of the structure develop. Only then can a more comprehensive grasp of the whole be attained.

It is useful to know, for example, that the narcissism in an adult, often regarded so pejoratively by his contemporaries, is charming in the normal two-year-old. In the child, narcissistic grandiosity cannot be self-sustaining; it reflects the child's participation in his perception of the adult's omnipotence and omniscience. Restating this in terms of ego psychology, the child's self representations cannot, at this point in his or her development, be clearly differentiated from the mental representations of the objects, and so the child participates in illusions of grandiosity supported by the daily shared delight in his or her own burgeoning capacities. This is not a game for the child, but a most serious task in development. If it persists and continues on into adulthood, however, it becomes pathological. That it is then phase-inappropriate is the tip of the iceberg, indicative of severe pathology of object relations beneath. Object representations have been decathected or negatively cathected, with the result that the self representations have taken the dominant position in the psychic structure. Wherever along the developmental continuum this takes place, the self representations are thereafter deprived of the modulating influence that more positive cathexes of the object representations would have exerted. The even distribution of cathexes between self and object representations, so essential for competent self and object relations, cannot be attained.

The thrust of this position is that all developmental processess are interdependent and interlocking. Therefore, to understand the individual, a dual approach is called for—first, evaluation of the total person in his or her specific environment at the moment, and second, understanding of the separate functioning aspects of the total structure, to be compared with and measured against a model of normal development. This has little to do with the taking of the usual psychosocial history. It refers to observation of the patient within the conceptual frame of reference provided by psychoanalytic developmental psychology.

The sixty-year-old patient who is engaged in a never-ending debate with an aged sibling over which one the parents of their childhood preferred is exhibiting a persistent need for the parental representations because the functions of evaluation and esteem have not been transferred to the self representations. It is not likely that, at this advanced age, such a developmental lag will be compensated for without therapeutic intervention.

The married couple who go through life as though they are bound together, engaging in little individual activity, reflect problems in adequate completion of the separation-individuation process.

The man who speaks of being very close to his sister, of loving her dearly, but who sees her every two years or so even though they are not far apart geographically, is informing the therapist about the state and quality of his capacity for object relations.

These examples may be viewed from the perspective of juxtaposing ego functions against a model of normal development of the whole person. It is not possible to diagnose developmental deficiency without taking into account that it has been incorporated, modified, defended against, in the total sweep of the organizing process. This highlights that no two borderline individuals are alike. One can, as Kernberg (1976) does, classify them as high, medium, or low level, on a scale. That manner of thinking is helpful but, taken alone, does not explain how it is that some psychotics as well as borderlines lead everyday lives without pathology that is apparent to the naked eye until serious stress situations expose the fragility of their structures.

Therefore, we continue to think along lines of specific functions, components, drives, and affects, and yet also attempt to include an orientation which views the total person. We believe, however, that we are far from the point at which we can understand the whole self because its innate complexities are so profound and intricate that there remains much more to be discovered about the component parts and their development. This is stated by Rangell:

> The whole works together in various degrees of harmony or disequilibrium. An abandonment of our knowledge of internal structure, however, with a return to a psychology of only the composite whole, is, in my opinion, a scientific regression rather than advance. What is lost is the explanatory reach amassed by total psychoanalytic theory, explanations of dreams, symptoms and character traits as compromise formation, the analysis of anxiety, conflicts and their derivation, the understanding of a phobia, an obsession, the structure of depression. (1982:869–870)

We would add that, while the whole person is more than the sum of the parts, the whole cannot be understood without a thoroughgoing understanding of the development of the parts.

CHAPTER 10
CONFLICT THEORY

F REUD'S WORK is best known for his discovery of the neuro-sogenic influence of wish, counterforce, conflict, defense, and symptom formation. At the time it was begun to be formulated in Freud's work from 1895 on, conflict theory represented a far more advanced alternative to the then-existing psychiatric theory of hereditary abnormality. At first conflict theory was a simple one of force and counterforce. With the introduction of the structural theory in 1923, the theory of conflict became far more sophisticated than its earlier version. To this day the psychoanalytic theory of neurosis remains a theory of conflict, and its explanatory literature, as we have shown, relies heavily upon military analogies. The superego wars with the id; sometimes superego and ego become allies; the ego is a battleground; the ego can also be a mediator; the id can overpower the ego; the superego can attack the ego. The oedipal conflict is usually depicted as one in which hostility and lust are more dominant than love, in which wishes to castrate and to murder motivate the action in the drama.

One reads of invading armies and attacking powers (A. Freud 1936). If the ego is powerful enough it forces the warring factions to compromise. Out of such strife the psyche is weakened; to avoid unbearable anxiety, energy must be expended in countercathexis. The ego, if competent enough, recognizes the anxiety as a signal and is capable of employing defenses against it. A compromise is effected between the two factions, permitting token gratification to each. This produces symptoms which result from the compromise and these symptoms, therefore, also represent the conflict. Often neurosis is asymptomatic; the result of the conflict is ego syntonic—that is, relatively comfortable for the individual because it has become part of the character. The rarity of disabling symptomatology these days as compared with Freud's time may account for the fact that some people are reluctant to seek out analysis even though those around them, more aware of the problems, recommend it to them.

The process whereby conflict results in compromise is obscured because it takes place unconsciously; only the symptoms, and often the incompletely repressed anxiety, are conscious. To maintain this arrangement in the unconscious, countercathectic energy must be continuously expended. The psychoanalytic process "lifts" the repression (the defense) by applying hypercathexis, thereby bringing the material into the preconscious, a step halfway between the unconscious and consciousness. When the movement from unconscious to preconscious is accomplished, interpretation brings the matter into consciousness.

The above describes the topographical theory and the concept of psychic energy. The topography of the psyche—conscious, preconscious, and unconscious—refers to three layers, and likens the psychoanalytic process to excavation. This theory preceded the structural theory and is believed by some (Arlow & Brenner 1964) to have been superseded by the structural theory. Most analysts are comfortable with both theories and do not find them incompatible but regard them, rather, as complementing one another.

Controversy is more widespread on the issue of psychic energy. It is assailed (more by academic psychologists than by psychoanalysts) because it does not follow the laws of modern physics regarding energy in general. Energic concepts, in Freud's day, followed hydrodynamic principles and are indeed outdated. But a more serious problem antedates modern physics. As important a theorist as Fenichel (1945) thought that deployment of countercathectic energy depletes physical energy. He carried his argument to the logical conclusion that persons suffering from neuroses are physically exhausted for the very reason that countercathectic energy is constantly expended. Observation does not bear him out. Except in depression, where there may be psychomotor retardation for other reasons, neurotics appear to maintain their physical capacities. This is especially so in obsessional neurosis where, despite the numerous defense mechanisms (repression, regression, reaction-formation, isolation, and undoing) and despite the complexity of the symptomatology, energy is available for real work. Fenichel fell into the fallacy of concretizing an abstraction, overlooking the fact that a construct is not a reality. One might even say that psychic energy does not exist, just as psychic structure does not exist except as an abstraction which serves to organize data.

There remain contradictions and omissions in conflict theory. How can the ego be battleground, participant, ally of the superego, as well as mediator of the conflict? How does the ego as mediator permit the warring factions token gratification in effecting a compromise? Is compromise the best and only solution to conflict? These questions remain unanswerable as long as the ego of the structural theory is endowed with more functions than such a construct can carry. It is for that reason that we reintroduce the concept of an overall executive apparatus, a superordinate ego. This relieves the ego of structure of the burden of being a battleground, a participant in the conflict, *and* the mediator of that conflict. The function of mediator, in particular, is better reserved for the executive agent, for it is that superordinate ego that carries out the functions of maintaining connections and ensuring the integrity of the entire personality. This conceptualization frees the ego of structure (adaptation in the narrow sense) to exercise its own functions which, especially since Hartmann, have become so familiar to us.

It is little recognized that there can be conflict before structuralization. One might ask how there can be, since the agencies that engage in conflict come into existence only after structure forms. Before structure is fully formed, ego and superego are not sufficiently developed to engage in the complex intersystemic conflict which characterizes the oedipal period. But the "simpler" conflicts of early development tax the personality as much or more than the later, more complex ones.

Mahler observes that there is an early conflictual state that precedes ambivalent object relations—ambitendency. This is a paradigm of early intersystemic conflict during the very process of structuralization. Her films show a toddler running up to a door through which the mother has just "disappeared." The child pushes up against the door and begins to cry, but is distracted by the observer who is offering a toy. Here there seems to be a wish for mother and a simultaneous wish to accept the toy and to be comforted by an other-than-mother. One may justifiably argue here that the ego is struggling with the id. The child wants and needs her mother, yet the ego functions of memory and anticipation combine with pleasure in the exercise of function to create just enough structure to counterbalance the need for connection with the primary object. For a while these are in exact balance; the toddler wants both at once and must go through the experience of finding that this is not possible. She falls into one or the other choice alternately until a balance begins to work its way into the psychic structure, enabling her to choose the one *or* the other.

This kind of conflict is vastly different from the more familiar intersystemic conflict of the oedipal crisis. We account for its omission from theory construction and for the emphasis upon oedipal conflict alone by the fact that, before child observation brought the developmental vicissitudes of preoedipal life into the mainstream of psychoanalytic thought, precise knowledge of preoedipal development was limited. The period of life before the oedipal conflict is reached was seen largely in psychosexual terms, even though Freud's writings mention object relations, mostly in passing.

It has been recognized for some time that consideration of psychosexual phases alone does not do justice to the complexity of early development. Jacobson noted that the oral phase encompasses far more than zonal activity; it includes all of the self and object experiences that take place in the larger constellation of the mother-child relationship—the maternal ministrations over and beyond feeding, such as warmth, cuddling, quickening of functions—and the child's interactions, such as entry into the dyadic relationship marked by imitation, vocalization, and registry of affective experiences. If development is to be explained in psychosexual terms, the oral phase has to be described in a way that encompasses entry into the first subphase of the separation-individuation process—differentiation. Also to be included are the indicators of the first organizer of the psyche (the smiling response) and of the second organizer (stranger anxiety, which marks the attainment of the libidinal object proper).

The second and third years of life correspond roughly with the anal and phallic phases of psychosexual development. There one would have to include burgeoning self and object images in an expanding object world, as well as the tasks of the practicing and rapprochement subphases; the acquisition of the third organizer (semantic communication); the progression of identification, internalization, structuralization; development of the defensive function of the ego; expanding object relationships on even higher, more internalized levels of object relations; the beginning of identity formation and approach to self and object constancy.

The term *preoedipal* is inadequate to describe the vast development now known in such exquisite detail. It merely connotes life before the oedipal period, but fails to encompass the details of early life, and it especially tends to deemphasize that that time of life consists of development that is crucial to the future mental life of the individual.

Inclusion of the object relations factor adds a large dimension to conflict theory. It describes the interpersonal exchanges and conflicts of the early months of life, and how these are formed into programs which have decisive effect upon the subsequent manner of negotiations with external objects, including the therapist. Freud began to take that factor into account when he noted that there is a reciprocal relationship between mother and child. By 1921 he was beginning to question whether psychosexuality is the only basis for object cathexis. He said then: "As a matter of fact we learn from psychoanalysis that there do exist other mechanisms for emotional ties, the so-called *identifications*" (p. 104).

Identification provides the basis for development of ever-higher levels of object relations by means of internalization. We have shown how the development of object relations begins at birth with the encounter between neonate and mothering person. By means of gradual internalization of self and object images throughout the early years of life, ever-higher degrees of structuralization are attained while the separation-individuation process moves the child toward self and object constancy.

Viewing the issue of conflict in developmental terms makes it clear that there is prestructural as well as structural conflict and that there are solutions other than compromise. More prevalent are the pathologies that are consequences of developmental and organizational failures, malformations in organization, such as the so-called borderline and narcissistic conditions and the character neuroses.

Conflict occurs as an aspect of structural differentiation. By the time of psychological birth the systems are sufficiently integrated to have evolved into a whole. We locate this level of integration at psychological

birth rather than following oedipal resolution for the reason that optimal oedipal resolution can be reached only by an already integrated
psychic system guided by the superordinate ego. While it remains
correct to say that a much higher order of structure evolves from oedipal
resolution, that can occur only where a level of structure capable of
dealing successfully with the stresses of the oedipal conflict is already
in place.

There is always an adaptive tendency despite structural deficiencies.
But adaptation in the absence of an ego capable of judgment and reality
testing is in the nature of an emergency measure which persists only
to become maladaptive later in life. Even though there is a level of
adaptive organization in spite of nurturing deficiencies, these inevitably
produce malformations such as excessive fantasy life, uncertain gender
identity, problems in identity formation in general. Except in psychosis,
the understructured as well as the structured personalities lead lives
that are less or more organized.

Even with maximum organization the id is still very much an integral part of life, with respect not only to the drives, but also to
fantasy, magical thinking, unconscious yearning, and the like. Without
these residues from the infantile period, life would be so totally rational
that it would be devoid of love and pleasure. But where the organizing
capacities are less secure, in the understructured personalities, mal-
adaptations are more prominent and intrude more into daily life and
functioning.

It adds substantially to the classical theory of neurosis to note that
there are qualitative and quantitative differences in object relations as
well as in all other features of the organizing process before and after
oedipal organization. Organization per se is the same process whether
it refers to the first organizer that integrates the primitive experiences
of the first few weeks of life, or to the second, third, and fourth
organizers (the Oedipus complex). Contained within the proposition of
a superordinate ego is the assumption that its manner of operation
remains the same whether it is integrating preoedipal or oedipal experience. Organization and structuralization are on a continuum. Oedipal organization, however, includes such substantially advanced
elements that quantity changes into quality. Thus one thinks quite

correctly of neurosis as something quite different from the pathologies which stem from earlier developmental failures.

Nevertheless, it serves to expand understanding of neurosis to classify it a consequence of developmental failure. Looked at in this way, neurosis represents failed object relations involving relationships among the self representations and the two sets of object representations in a struggle that, for optimal mental health, must be resolved in favor of accepting one's generational fate. Inclusion of the object relations factor alters the traditional view that oedipal solution short of resolution comes about as a result of compromise effected by the ego as mediator. Now one must think that it comes about by means of alteration among the self and object representations as the child in the triad modifies his or her self representation to conform with the reality that he or she is a child, incapable of adult sexuality.

Also modified are the ideas about murderous and castrating wishes. These have to be thought of as attenuated and counterbalanced by long-standing positive cathexis of both sets of parental representations. An oedipal boy who has a history of object connection with a loving father going back to the first year of life cannot, at the oedipal phase, long sustain a wish to murder. Nor can he long sustain the thought of the formerly loving father as a castrator even where this represents projection of his own covetous wishes toward the father's superior phallus.

Since some sort of neurotic solution remains the fate of most survivors of early childhood who are fortunate enough to escape more severe pathology, we are forced to look more deeply into neurosogenesis. In that examination, the roles of the three agencies of structure have to be reviewed in the light of our proposal that theory is strengthened if certain so-called ego functions are carried out by a superordinate ego which acts as a central steering organization.

The components of neurosis can be broken down into the following elements:

1. Wish
2. Fear of consequences
3. Anxiety
4. Ego as battleground

5. Ego as mediator
6. Ego in its defensive function
7. Compromise
8. Symptom formation

1. Wish

Before the child has to deal with the full force of the oedipal wish, he or she has already experienced drive opposition. The first is weaning, followed by toilet training. These involve object relations more complex and interactive than cursory thought would suggest. The helpless child has to yield to the arbitrarily imposed wishes of the powerful adult. But in optimal circumstances, weaning and toilet training are accomplished in interaction between child and "aggressor." The child yields to weaning as much because oral needs are waning as because it is willed upon the child by the weaner, if timing is sensitive and if the relationship is in positive balance. Toilet training is a somewhat more complex version of a similar process. If sufficient gratification of anal needs has been permitted, that need also wanes. But by this time a level of self and object relations obtains that offers the child little or no choice. Because optimal organization includes object cathexis, the child cannot persist in seeking zonal gratification in disregard for the object. Therefore, it is not likely that the child will choose gratification of zonal needs at the expense of the essential and more gratifying object connection. That connection allows for identification with parental values and also allows the formation of images of a good, functioning, pleasing, loved, and loving self. At this stage of development, long before oedipal object relations are timely, there is potential for difficulty that may burden oedipal resolution when that time arrives. Object relations difficulties that have their inception earlier in life hamper progression to genital primacy.

It has always been implied that a rather high level of object relations must obtain for genital primacy to be reached. Long before ego psychology and the object relations theory that stems from it had become formalized, psychoanalytic theory brought together psychosexuality and object relations as convergent aspects of genital primacy. It proposed that, at that highest psychosexual level, zonal need and need for object connection include regard for the object as well. Deficiencies in self and object esteem hinder development by promoting continued clinging to pregenital zonal gratifications which are less object oriented. Continuation of autoerotic activity beyond age-appropriate time is an example of perseverance in zonal modes which dominates over object connection.

Experiences which build frustration tolerance and anxiety tolerance strengthen the child for the oedipal struggle. The role of the parental objects before the oedipal crisis is to help the child attain frustration tolerance, anxiety tolerance, awareness of reality and conformity to it, all within the context of comfortably attuned self and object experience at every step. The role of the child with adequate endowment, including the important capacity to extract from the environment, is to fit together with the environment and to organize the increasing numbers of components of development as they compound daily. By the time of the oedipal crisis, the well-enough developing child has already built a structure molded by reality testing and including patterns of relating to self and object representations which assure the child a place in the world. Even under such optimal circumstances the oedipal position is difficult. But taming influences and coping capacities are by then internalized and will not be lost in the crucible of the oedipal crisis.

Where disorganization that makes for neurosis dominates, negative self and object experiences have preceded the oedipal situation and make for disarray and malformation in organization. Mahler's observational studies show that, with adequate rapprochement experience, severe neurosis may be averted. One of the compelling forces in rapprochement is the child's awareness that he or she is a very small person in a very large world. Reality testing of this profound order can be achieved only where the separation-individuation process has proceeded solidly enough to enable the child to surrender belief in parental omnipotence comfortably. It is comfortable because, with the transfer of the functions of the object representations to the self representation, need for parental omnipotence diminishes. Attainment of this degree of reality testing impels the child to abandon the grandiosity of the practicing subphase, and to seek reunion with a stronger person, a protecting parent, but one who is no longer needed as omnipotent. It is not likely that the sobering effect of reality testing will be lost unless rapprochement disappointment forces the child to regress to the omnipotence of the practicing subphase. But with adequate rapprochement, the child approaches the oedipal phase with awareness that he or she is still a child and, as such, an unequal partner in the oedipal configuration.

We see the developing years as providing competence to deal with future crises—the Oedipus complex, adolescence, and the other critical periods throughout the life cycle. Disorganization, which may make its first appearance at the oedipal level, in latency, in adolescence, or even in adulthood, is built upon malformations that have their inception in earlier levels of object relations. In those circumstances, the oedipal crisis leads to neurosis at best, or to regression to less than neurotic borderline and narcissistic conditions if the degree of organization cannot support and sustain the personality at the higher level.

Organization may be so malformed that the oedipal level cannot be reached competently. The classical neuroses, viewed in this light, represent failure in organization. The superordinate ego does not succeed in its role of guiding all components into a harmonious whole. Failure is of the totality of organization. It prevents some individuals from reaching the oedipal level, while others limp into that developmental position so handicapped by earlier failure that oedipal resolution is not possible without therapeutic intervention.

The more traditional view of this state of affairs is that the id overthrows the ego. In the broadest sense, that is correct. The more precise way of describing that situation is that the elements to be organized are already so skewed that the superordinate ego cannot bring them into comfortable equilibrium. The resultant shaky balance depends heavily upon symptoms to maintain an uneasy stability.

2. Fear of Consequences

As is so well known, Freud thought that the boy's choice in the oedipal dilemma is to pursue his wish and risk castration or to relinquish the wish. Freud found no comparable incentive for the girl to relinquish the oedipal wish; he concluded, therefore, that she does not complete that task and is left with a less adequate superego. Current thinking about female psychology acknowledges that Freud's inferences about female development constitute the weakest part of his theoretical structure. For the most part, however, reviews of Freud's thinking about female development omit his 1933 lecture on female sexuality, where he modifies his earlier thoughts about activity and passivity, asserting now that these are unrelated to gender. His earlier attempts to bring sexual development and gender identity into conformity with drive theory had led him to some untenable conclusions. But by 1933 he says:

> That is all I had to say to you about femininity. It is certainly incomplete and fragmentary and does not always sound friendly. But do not forget that I have only been describing women in so far as their nature is determined by their sexual function. It is true that that influence extends very far; but we do not overlook the fact that an individual woman may be a human being in other respects as well. If you want to know more about femininity, enquire from your own experiences of life, or turn to the poets, or wait until science can give you deeper and more coherent information. (1933b:135)

It is now proven (Jacobson, Mahler, Galenson & Roiphe) that "castration shock" is experienced by both sexes earlier than at the phallic phase. The castration threat is an endopsychic one. In the rare instances in which a father actually threatens his son with castration, much more primitive wishes exist on both sides of an already impaired object relationship with a cruel father. A normal, loving father supports his son's masculinity and offers himself for identification. The traditional view that the oedipal boy fears his father's retaliation in more than a fleeting way is not consistent with contemporary object relations theory, for it assumes that son and father (as well as daughter and mother) have no history of positive interaction which has established positively cathected object representations. Object relations theory suggests that it is this positive balance, "in the black," which carries child and parent through the child's oedipal crisis. (See chapter 11.)

A similar argument holds for the wish to murder the parent of the same sex. Death wishes are an aspect of childhood fantasy life. Ambivalence, by definition, includes loving as well as hostile feelings toward the same person. There is a tendency to adultomorphize the extent and quality of a child's murderous wishes. Freud observed that an "extreme and unmeasured intensification of every emotion" (1921:78) is a feature of childhood. The fact of death is difficult even for adults to grasp. To a child death is reversible, and death wishes exist only at given moments, at the height of hostile affect. Where death wishes dominate throughout, there is something seriously wrong in the object relationship. Normally, love overrides hostility, and the child who wishes the parent "dead" at one moment wishes him or her alive at the next.

There are other deterrents to the pursuit of raw oedipal wishes. The oedipal child with competent reality testing knows that he or she is not yet equipped to fulfill adult roles, neither in the purely sexual sense because of biological incapacity, nor in the broader roles of husband or wife. Oedipal wishes undoubtedly place the child in conflict, but there is an unfortunate tendency to view such wishes differently from the way in which other childhood wishes are regarded. Normally, they exist within the context of a deeply dependent relationship with two benignly disposed adults. Ultimately, as Jacobson has pointed out, oedipal relinquishment is accomplished because love for the parent of the same sex as well as reality testing dominate sexual drive. Then the child can be said to join his or her own generation.

3. Anxiety

The structural theory and its elaboration in *Inhibitions, Symptoms, and Anxiety* (Freud 1926a) extend consideration of anxiety beyond castration. Anxiety, Freud proposes there, is the consequence of intersystemic tension. Whether it can be experienced as a signal depends upon the capacity of the ego to limit anxiety to signal status in the first place and, in the second, upon the existence of an organization adequate enough to use the signal to employ defenses. This assumes that there has been a gradual development of anxiety tolerance in the ongoing process of organization, beginning with memory traces of relief from hunger that enable the infant to learn to wait for the next feeding. This means that anxiety can be tolerated if object images remain reliable. In fact, in tolerable doses, anxiety and frustration are essential to motivate the child to find his or her own resources and to promote the separation-individuation process.

The capacity to soothe oneself, acquired by the transfer of that function from the object representation to the self representation, is a precursor to the development of anxiety tolerance and the capacity to reduce anxiety to a signal. Because of the affective experience of having been soothed, the child has relatively long experience with anxiety in tolerable amounts before the very great anxiety of the oedipal conflict threatens. To have to cope with this greater anxiety strains the organization to the utmost.

Here the utility of the concept of a superordinate ego is again illustrated. The ego of structure experiences anxiety, reduces it to a signal, and defends against it. These functions keep it "busy" enough. It is left to the superordinate ego to maintain the integrity and stability of the entire structure as the ego endures the strain of the wish, counterforce, anxiety, and solution or resolution. Whether the solution is neurosis with or without symptom formation, or regressive abandonment of the oedipal position, is determined in large measure by competence in dealing with anxiety gained from earlier self and object experience. Confident persons who have internalized safety feelings will be able to endure more anxiety than those whose levels of organization have not included that important component in sufficient quantity.

In the final analysis, anxiety is an affect that remains as a potential thoughout life and makes itself felt at critical moments. Its function is often lifesaving and does not cripple or otherwise impair the total organization if it remains at less than phobic levels. Where phobias or similar symptoms emerge, it is because they have been incorporated within the organization as the best solution or compromise possible at the time. What is compromised, looked upon in this light, is optimal organizational competence because the component parts consist of elements such as poor anxiety tolerance, low levels of internalized safety feelings, impaired self-images, or unreliable object images. This is another way of stating that the superordinate ego arranges the best possible adaptation, but that it can use only the material at hand.

4. Ego as Battleground

It is inconsistent with the definition of ego to designate it as a battleground. As a coherent organization of mental processes, it would lose coherence if subverted to battleground use. As a process of organization (1979), organizing would cease while battles are being waged because this function would be impaired by the chaos of battle.

But such arguments do not resolve the issue, for it was not without purpose that the ego was described as a battleground. It was necessary to account for the fact that conflict does take place, and it aids conceptualization to provide a locus. Acknowledging that, we are left to wonder whether locus is essential to the vast abstraction that is psychic structure. It seems to us that not much is lost by dispensing with it. To be able to visualize the ego as a passive field of battle between id and superego is small gain for reducing it to such passivity. And it remains contradictory to visualize it as a battleground, participant in the struggle, and mediator.

It has long been considered unnecessary to locate the psyche in the brain or in the mind. Since our main thrust is to relieve the ego of unnecessary conceptual burden, we are comfortable in thinking about conflict as waged without specific locus. If locus aids conceptualization, one might say that conflict takes place in the "space" between the systems. To relieve the ego of unnecessary conceptual burden frees it to participate in conflict, to limit the anxiety aroused by conflict, to defend, and to organize on the narrow level of daily experience.

5. Ego as Mediator

In addition to defense, the ego, by the time of the oedipal crisis, has become competent in delay, in controlling impulse discharge, in frustration tolerance, and, as already discussed, in anxiety reduction. One can argue that impulses are controlled by mediation, but this gets close to the battleground metaphor. Can the ego be assailed by impulse and at the same time function as mediator, participant, bystander, and battleground?

6. Ego in Its Defensive Function

Since Freud (1923–26), and especially Anna Freud (1936), established that it is the function of a strong enough ego to employ defenses and defense mechanisms, this became a key position in the psychoanalytic theory of neurosis. It remained for Hartmann and Jacobson to suggest alterations and modifications. The concept of change in function (Hartmann) wrests defense from its status as energic drain on the resources of the psyche by proposing that it can also serve adaptation. Consistent with our proposition that the superordinate ego rather than the ego, as Hartmann proposed, is the "organ of adaptation," all defenses, whether countercathectic or liberated, are adaptive in the sense that adaptation is the best equilibrium the process of organization can achieve at every given point in development.

Jacobson elaborates on the concept of change in function using the example of reaction-formation. While reaction-formation remains a defense mechanism, it often changes in function and thereby promotes a fundamental change in the personality as a whole, altering basic attitudes toward self and object representations. The first direction of reaction-formation is against the drives. With change in function it alters in quality to become character traits that serve the higher levels of functioning—traits such as orderliness and logical thinking which reinforce the secondary process.

To think of defense as adaptive, as the best adjustment possible under the circumstances, assigns the overall adaptive function or, we might say, the long run adaptive function to the superordinate ego. This relegates to the ego the function of immediate and sometimes emergency employment of defense and, if available, defense mechanisms. The superordinate ego, which assures the overall stability of the defense of the psyche as a whole, determines whether defenses instituted at one time remain adaptive for the lifetime. If they have become maladaptive, it is sometimes possible, without therapy, for the individual to change their form as well as their function. With therapy, the very purpose may be described in terms of changing maladaptive to adaptive functioning.

7. *Compromise*

Compromise can be effected only where there is compelling influence which can be brought to bear upon the conflicting parties. The compromise solution, therefore, forces acceptance of a broader overall perspective rather than continuation of the conflict on the narrower issues around which both parties to the conflict are in contention. Traditionally, it is believed that one of the parties—the ego—enforces compromise. We have shown that this is not a viable position if it is also assumed that the ego is a participant in the conflict. Our suggestion is that the matter be viewed more broadly, from a vantage point that takes into account both libidinal need to retain connection and aggressive drive urgency to protect identity and autonomy. This broader perspective is within the purview of the superordinate ego which we regard as the agency capable of enforcing solutions, not compromise alone. Latency, for example, represents postponement of sexuality and the conflicts surrounding it. This is not compromise, but may be thought of as "buying" developmental time until the individual acquires greater competency, both psychological and biological.

8. Symptom Formation

Diagnosis is to be established, not from the symptom, but from the structure of the ego in which the symptom is embedded (Eissler 1953). To this date, more than thirty years later, this has still not been given its deserved emphasis in some quarters. In the *Diagnostic and Statistical Manual* of the American Psychiatric Association (DSM-III 1980), widely used for diagnostic classification, this is entirely ignored. Eissler's purpose is to draw attention to the level of total organization—the whole rather than that part of the whole represented by the compromise. Diagnosis by symptom has also been challenged on the ground that similar symptomatology, such as phobic or hysterical formations, can appear at all levels of structuralization (Wangh 1959; Rangell 1959). Depression is another example; it may appear in any part of the diagnostic spectrum and provides no clue, in and of itself, to the nature of the structure in which it is embedded. (See also chapter 12.)

Freud, in distinguishing transference neuroses from the narcissistic neuroses, emphasized the decisive aspect of object relations as a factor of greater prognostic importance than the specific symptomatology of the several kinds of neuroses. His focus, too, was on the whole person within the fundamental frame of reference of object relations, in that instance whether cathexis is self-directed or object directed. Seventy years after his "Introduction" to the study of narcissism, never completed, he remains essentially correct in regarding the "narcissistic neuroses" as untreatable because object cathexis is not available. It is only by virtue of the most recently acquired information about the nature of borderline and narcissistic structures that we are able to understand pathological narcissism somewhat better and to see gradations within a spectrum that ranges from permeable (treatable) narcissistic formations to impermeable ones.

CHAPTER 11

TRIADIC OBJECT RELATIONS: THE OEDIPUS COMPLEX

OUR PURPOSE here is to show that the complexities of the oedipal situation can be more broadly comprehended by combining the theories of psychosexual maturation, structuralization, and conflict with the object relations theory derived from ego psychology. We believe that this will enrich conceptual thinking about the manner in which sexuality (from drive theory) and love (from object relations theory) connect at the oedipal position.

The implications of emphasizing this dramatic convergence are broad. They are especially enlightening in their contribution to understanding the incompetent oedipal arrangements of the less adequately structured personalities. In these pathologies, if the oedipal position is at all approached, it is distorted and incomplete because of the very failure of the convergence of drive with the corresponding level of object relations. Here we shall combine psychoanalytic object relations theory with the first developmental theory of psychoanalysis, psychosexual maturation.

This is not altogether new. Those who preceded us were remarkably successful despite the fact that they lacked the knowledge of object relations which we possess today. It is for that reason that those contributions must now be updated. Although Freud had object relations in mind from the beginning of his work, it was not until 1940 and after that others began to consider the interrelatedness of drive and object relations as they affect the oedipal position, and especially to note the importance of preoedipal object relations.

In 1952 J. Lampl de Groot elaborated upon Freud's 1905 statement about the importance of the object, showing in particular how the Oedipus complex develops from the preoedipal relationship with the mother, and restating that which Freud had already mentioned—that differences in the nature of the early mother attachments manifest themselves not only in the oedipal relationships, but also in adult object relationships. She referred to the Oedipus complex as the final product of preoedipal development, emphasizing that disturbances in the preoedipal phase can cause abnormal shapes and weaknesses in the oedipal constellation.

Gitelson was also interested in the effect of preoedipal life upon the Oedipus complex, although he referred to it as *pregenital* because he wrote in a period of psychoanalytic theory construction when *pregenital* (which refers to psychosexuality) and *preoedipal* (which refers to the object relations line of development) were used interchangeably. It is clear that Gitelson wished to refer to *preoedipal* factors because he went on to make the exceedingly important point that, in borderline and psychotic conditions, no more than a vestigial oedipal position can be reached because "object relations were destroyed, root and branch, at an earlier period, or because such relations never existed at all" (1952:353).

Analysts are still struggling to integrate drive theory with ego psychological object relations theory, and so they refer to the preoedipal period of life as pregenital. Lebovici refers to "pregenital organization in object relationships" (1982:205) although pregenitality is not an organizer. It is but one of the many features of development that the superordinate ego is required to organize. The psychosexual level, the level and quality of self and object relations, the capacities of the innate endowment, the quality of the life experience before the "moment" under consideration, the resultant of interaction, the rigidity or flexibility of the fixed assumptions, all become organized under the aegis of the superordinate ego.

To attain the objective of describing the confluence of drive and level of object relations, especially as it pertains to the complete Oedipus complex, we extend Spitz's (1959) concept of critical periods. Spitz's concern is with the first eighteen months of life. The concept itself, however, is equally valuable in contributing to a more thorough understanding of the convergence of psychosexual maturation and object relations at the oedipal level because that developmental phenomenon also fits Spitz's definition of a critical period. Rangell (1972), in a similar vein, extends another of Spitz's concepts—the organizers of the psyche—to oedipal phenomena; he suggests that the Oedipus complex is the fourth in the series of organizers of the psyche.

Freud introduced the hyphenated term "phallic-oedipal" in 1905 to describe the psychosexual and object relations position of the child entering the oedipal phase. And in 1924 he maintained that the phallic phase is contemporaneous with the oedipal position. He believed that the genital phase is not attained in the infantile period, but that sexual development is interrupted by latency, and that genitality is reached after that. While that formulation was adequate for its time, it seems desirable now to regard the phallic phase as pregenital and to think that a first approach to genitality which we (1979) term *genital interest* is made in the infantile period. This reasoning is central to our thesis, namely that genitality and object love are the essential components of the Oedipus complex. We suggested that genital interest, a precursor of true genitality, has the status of the fourth psychosexual phase of the infantile period. At this level, the same bodily organ that is used in the phallic phase is now cathected in a new way, no longer solely for narcissistic pleasure, but for object-related pleasure. We say:

> A position not based solely upon anatomy would include psychological development as well as physical maturation. Then, discovery of the genitalia *and* of autonomous functioning can be seen as constituting determinants of identity formation and simultaneously as furthering the separation process, the complementary track of the individuation process. From this we may conclude that interest in one's genitals at the so-called phallic phase represents, for both sexes, a beginning culmination of the connection to the symbiotic object and to symbiotic need. It is at this point in development that aggressive drive comes into dominance as a separating and individuating force. That part of the anatomy that will later be used by the libidinal drive to seek connection is used also by the aggressive drive to preserve ego boundaries by establishing gender interest and gender difference. (1979:85)

This formulation preserves the object relations aspect of the oedipal situation, which is lost if the oedipal position is combined with a pregenital psychosexual phase. More important, however, the role of autonomous functioning in development is stressed. This may contribute toward filling in one of the "blank spaces" in psychoanalytic theory by proposing a solution to the puzzle of the shift in the object at the oedipal level, especially for the girl. It implies that both boy and girl find their heterosexual destinies in the progressive development of autonomous functioning, which joins the nonhostile aggressive drive in propelling the individual toward ever-higher levels of development. The shift in the object has been stressed in the literature as essential for the girl if she is to attain the oedipal position. But as we consider that the shift is also from passive to active in relation to the object, it becomes clear that the boy, too, has to make an important shift in the juxtaposition of self and object representations. That the object in reality is the same person for the boy at both the oedipal and preoedipal levels is merely an external, not an intrapsychic, fact.

The phallic phase, on the other hand, more resembles the pregenital phases that precede it—that is, cathexis of the erogenous zone for narcissistic rather than for object-directed pleasure remains dominant. This dominance has a fluctuating quality throughout the phases of pregenitality as the child learns to tame drive needs to conform with developing object relations. Dominance of object relations over drive is first experienced in the anal phase, while in the phallic phase there is a reversal. We shall elaborate upon this important theme shortly.

Edgcumbe and Burgner recognize the theoretical incompatibility of joining the phallic phase with the oedipal position. They point out that the assumption that the oedipal child is at the same time a phallic child is a legacy from the historical growth of psychoanalytic theory. They say:

> Our examination of the literature disclosed a tendency to assume that entry into the phallic phase is accompanied by the *simultaneous development* of oedipal object relationships, so that the terms phallic, oedipal, and phallic-oedipal are often used synonymously. *Yet close scrutiny of clinical and observational material reveals distinct differences in the forms of drive derivatives and in the nature of the child's relationships in the preoedipal phallic phase as compared with the phallic-oedipal phase.* (1975:162; italics theirs)

We can agree with them in recognizing the awkward theoretical contradiction in equating phallic and oedipal, but we find the solution that they suggest—to postulate that there are two phallic phases, one oedipal and the other preoedipal—to be equally awkward. We suggest, instead, that approach to genitality does not await termination of latency to make its first appearance.

Galenson and Roiphe (1976, 1980) question whether there is a phallic phase in girls. Although the issue is not resolved, it is clear from newly discovered knowledge about female psychology that the girl's phallic phase, if it exists, must be quite different from that of the boy. Jacobson, borne out by the later investigation of Galenson and Roiphe, shows that awareness of anatomical difference is forced upon the child's attention, not at the phallic phase as Freud thought, but in the second year of life. This finding necessitates consideration of the resonating effect of this dramatic discovery upon the phallic phase proper when that phase is reached. The phallic phase must be appreciably shaped and influenced by the earlier discovery and by the quality of recovery from the impact of it.

We have shown how, from the beginning of extrauterine life, zonal need begins to become organized with experience of gratification, and how internalization begins. As early as 1905 Freud knew that the first affective experiences of a gratified self become the template for future gratification. Quickened by maternal stimulation in the oral phase, the pleasure-seeking aims permeate subsequent psychosexual phases as these mature in conjunction with ego development, orchestrated by the organizing process. Organization becomes increasingly complex as psychosexual maturation and ego development proceed. By the anal phase, self and object images are more differentiated than before; object relations have expanded to include father, siblings, and others; motor skills have increased and fall under the control of the total ego organization. Transfer of erogeneity from the oral to the anal zone brings the child into a situation in which gratification of drive needs and of object need come into opposition. The child must learn to subordinate the drive in order to comply with the wishes of the much-needed object. This is well known. What we wish to add is that here exists the first precursor of genitality—where sexual need is conjoined with object love. The second precursor will be established when drive need and object relations coincide at the oedipal level. At the anal level the pattern for combining psychosexuality with object love is established by means of the suppression of direct discharge, which, in the oral phase, was carried out without regard for the object. Later, reaction-formation supersedes suppression as drive opposition to comply with object need becomes part of structure and even acquires secondary autonomy.

The ego functions of anticipation, delay, and intentionality were begun to be acquired in the oral phase. When the capacity for sphincter control is added, intentionality broadens in scope to become volition. Now the child is on the way to exercising ego autonomy, which begins with the well-known "No" (Spitz 1957). "Yes" becomes possible when identification with the aggressor undergoes a change in function (Hartmann 1939), making it possible to agree without loss of autonomy. The very style of achieving pleasure begins to shift from self-directed to object directed. However, if this is not to be pathologically altruistic, there must be a gratifying return. Thus, while still in the anal phase, the child discovers that pleasure can be attained by the use of the body to please the object, and that that pleasure can be greater than that of pleasing oneself alone. In well-conducted training the child is, of course, not required to abandon zonal gratification entirely, only to bend it to the wishes of the object. Thus the pleasure-seeking attitude first acquired in the oral phase gains reinforcement in the next phase and continues, despite regression during the phallic phase, through the psychosexual progression.

With this major shift from drive dominance to compromise with object relations need in the anal phase, the form and direction of object relations alter. From that time on, the wish to give pleasure while receiving begins to enter the character.

At the phallic phase the capacity for compromising drive need with object cathexis appears to undergo a regression. Cathexis of the erogenous zone once again dominates, subordinating object need. Return to a more narcissistic cathexis of the body is an essential step for the consolidation of bodily integrity before the child can once again, as in the anal phase, subordinate drive needs by effecting a compromise between them and regard for the object. In this way the self representation is secured and more even cathexis between self and object representations can ensue. Then, transfer to genital interest combined with object love moves the child into the oedipal position proper.

While this is taking place on the side of the drives, ego development is proceeding. Especially in the practicing subphase of the separation-individuation process, which is simultaneous with the anal phase, certain personality characteristics are acquired which also contribute to later oedipal competence. We are proposing that traits such as venturesomeness, initiative, courage, and even ambition are developed in an adequate practicing subphase and that these predispose to the ability to enter the very center of the oedipal conflict and, in favorable circumstances, even to conquer it. Traits such as indecision, hesitancy, timidity, fearfulness—consequences of an inadequate practicing subphase, impair the ability to deal with the oedipal crisis.

The oedipal level of object relations is most desirably attained after the practicing and rapprochement subphases, when interpersonal relationships have given way to intrasystemic negotiations between self and object representations, and when structuralization has proceeded far enough to make intersystemic conflict possible.

Pursuing the theme that the oedipal level is a critical period, representing convergence of drive maturation and ego development, one has to think about it as occurring over a span of time, even in the first round. The entry point, middle phase, and temporary cessation of oedipal wishes that take place with entry into latency differ in quality and intensity. That oedipal wishes revive again in adolescence, early adulthood, parenthood, and perhaps even later in the life cycle has been pointed out by several authors (Blos 1962; Benedek 1959; Blanck & Blanck 1968).

In normal sequential development, the oedipal position is attained after or in coincidence with psychological birth—that is, when the child is on the way to object constancy. Freud describes the complete Oedipus complex:

> One gets an impression that the simple Oedipus complex is by no means its commonest form, but rather represents a simplification or schematization which, to be sure, is often enough justified for practical purposes. Closer study usually discloses the more complete Oedipus complex, which is twofold, positive and negative, and is due to the bisexuality originally present in children: that is to say, a boy has not merely an ambivalent attitude towards his father and an affectionate object-choice towards his mother but at the same time he also behaves like a girl and displays an affectionate feminine attitude towards his father and a corresponding jealousy and hostility towards his mother. (1923:33)

Freud worded this as though it is an interpersonal conflict, although it is generally understood that this conflict really exists in internalized form, not between the oedipal child and parent, but intersystemically between id and superego, and intrasystemically between self and object representations.

To understand the Oedipus complex in modern terms, revision of the universally accepted diagram of an equilateral triangle is in order. That diagram is misleading, not only because it suggests that the three participants in the oedipal drama are on equal terms, but also because it fails to depict the negative as well as the positive position with the accuracy now made possible by contemporary theory. While diagrams cannot do justice to the complex psychological constructs we attempt to illustrate with them, they do aid in conceptualization if we do not take them too literally. We propose a straight line instead of a triangle, with one parent representation at either pole, while the oedipal child moves along the line flexibly. This makes it possible to visualize her or him closer to one parent representation at one psychological moment, to the other parent representation at another moment, and in the very middle of the conflict at still another time. These variations in position depict the negative as well as the positive oedipal situations. If we wish to be even more precise, we may imagine a calibrated line which can tell exactly where the self representation of the oedipal child stands in relation to the object representations at any given psychological moment.

At the point of entry the oedipal strivings have a fleeting quality because they are in a state of flux before coming firmly into the oedipal position proper. The developing child may at one moment "touch" the oedipal position and may, at another moment, regress to a preoedipal level of object need. Whether regression is along the psychosexual line as well, that is, to phallic, anal, or even oral levels, can only be determined in individual cases. These fluctuations are determined by the state of object need and, where there is defensive regression, by the level of anxiety. The child, whether boy or girl, may at one moment be in the position of needing the maternal object in one representational form, as an oedipal object, and at another moment need the same person in the entirely different representational form of the object of a lower developmental level of object need.

For those reasons, then, the concept of the negative oedipal position calls for reexamination. Our line of reasoning thus far leads to the conclusion that the oedipal level is competently reached when the level of object relations and the coinciding psychosexual level converge to form the complete Oedipus complex. This implies that the child cannot be in a passive position in relation to either parent if it is to be said that she or he is in the oedipal position proper.

Clinical observation appears to refute this. In the course of an analysis, one sees the patient in an apparently passive position in relation to the parent of the same sex as a defense against oedipal anxiety. This poses neither a theoretical nor a clinical dilemma. Clinically, the determination is made according to the nature and quality of that special object relationship that we call transference, the reflection of the object relations of the infantile neurosis. Careful attention to the level of object relations contributes to clinical precision, especially in the interpretation of that which is truly oedipal, by distinguishing the transference manifestations in terms of object need.

The so-called negative oedipal position resembles the structure of obsessional neurosis in reverse. In that neurosis, regression is along the psychosexual line to the anal position, while the foothold in the oedipal level of object relations is retained. In the complete Oedipus complex, the psychosexual position is retained while, under the pressure of anxiety, there may be regression along the object relations line to the haven of preoedipal, dyadic, object relations.

We turn now to the myth as dramatized by Sophocles. Van der Sterren (1952) analyzed it as one would a dream, to expose the latent content. His purpose was to show that Oedipus was motivated by hostility toward his mother for having abandoned him. One can agree with that. To be added are the affective tones of the oedipal situation, especially the split affects and split object images. There are the images of a destructive father, as well as of a loving father in the forms of the shepherd and the foster father. The quantitative distribution between positive and negative object images is a preponderance of negative images. This suggests a pause for careful consideration of such easily arrived-at conjectures as projection of the son's hostility, for the neonate is a blank slate so far as object images are concerned. In the myth, hostile paternal object images abound. These always have a prehistory, as J. M. Ross (1982) points out in describing Laius' own history of abandonment and persecution.

To our way of thinking, Jocasta was the guiltier parent. Not only did she share in the abandonment, she chose a destructive father for her child; she could not function as an adequate preoedipal mother whose role in such circumstances would have been, not only the usual one of the good enough mother of the preoedipal period, but also as protector against the father's hostility. Further, she failed to maintain the generation gap and the incest taboo.

Thus the Oedipus myth does not describe a normal family situation, although Freud applies it to normal development. The normal oedipal situation requires that there shall have been a preoedipal family life in which preponderantly positive self and object representations develop out of positive affective experiences. These attenuate the murderous wishes of the oedipal phase. We have already questioned whether the normally developing child can sustain the wish to kill the parent of the same sex with whom she or he has built up positive cathexes over the preoedipal years. Such wishes have to be transient, not even necessarily restricted to oedipal wishes, but more broadly attributable to normal negative affect and ambivalence. We are not persuaded that the oedipal wish can overthrow all that went before, although its power must be acknowledged. Further, it is usually insufficiently emphasized that the oedipal child has acquired a sense of time which includes the fantasy of "when I grow up." The fantasy yields to the phase-specific sense of reality that develops in later years. We follow Jacobson in her assertion that love for the parent of the same sex results in identification rather than destruction.

Many hostile-appearing behaviors are construed as such because of the confusion between aggression (a drive) and hostility (an affect) (Freud 1940; Blanck & Blanck 1979). With regard to all developmental thrusts, including the oedipal one, we have to distinguish between those that represent object-directed hostility and those that emanate from the growth-promoting aspects of the aggressive drive. The oedipal child who wishes to supplant the parent of the same sex is expressing wishes of the same nature and quality as the younger child who wants to do for himself or herself what has been done by the parent. By means of the transfer of functions of the object representations to the self representation, a developmental thrust takes place that is too often misconstrued as destructively object directed. It is true that the developing child can become quite hostile in an object-directed way, especially if the developmental thrusts are impeded by an unattuned parent. This has to be distinguished from the thrust itself which is powered by normal, nonhostile aggression.

The oedipal level of object relations is, by Freud's very designation, more complex than earlier levels. Nevertheless, it does not differ from them qualitatively if we think about thrust toward autonomy. The complexity enters because the object relations have shifted from predominantly dyadic to definitely triadic, and because the child is not yet physiologically equipped to carry out his or her sexual wishes. These are aspects of the human condition which make us prone to neurosis.

As Loewald (1979) points out, many terms have been applied to the puzzle of how the Oedipus complex is surmounted. The Brill translation of the *Collected Papers* refers to the passing of the Oedipus complex. *The Standard Edition* translates it as dissolution. Sometimes it is referred to as destruction. More commonly, one speaks of resolution. Loewald uses the more felicitous term *waning* to reflect the contemporary view that it never disappears altogether. Sometimes one hears of the child's oedipal defeat. In the case of a genius, such as Picasso, one hears of the father's defeat by the son, based simply on the fact that the father ceased painting when he recognized his son's greater talent. Our alternate interpretation of this is that the father was a growth promoter.

It is, of course, fallacious to regard victory or defeat in the oedipal situation in externalized or interpersonal terms. If the outcome of the oedipal conflict were to be regarded as a defeat in reality, the result would be a person who forever after fears to venture. As we shall discuss in chapter 16, there are some who regard all analyses as unterminated because the oedipal wish is unconsummated. This focuses on defeat rather than the fact that the very victory in the conquest of oedipal wishes promotes growth through structuralization, especially the formation of a discrete superego.

If there were truly defeat in the failure to consummate oedipal wishes, all of the traits that we suggest are the consequence of adequate practicing subphase experience would be lacking later in life—venturesomeness, initiative, ambition, courage. It is because the conflict is an intrapsychic one that must be resolved in favor of living in one's own generation that victory builds structure. The outcome, at the least, is the compromise of neurotic formation. At most, ego and superego gain strength from having joined forces. The victory is that the final stage of structuralization is attained—cohesion of the disparate superego components into a distinct structure.

Loewald believes, as do we, that understanding preoedipal issues will contribute to a broader insight into oedipal issues. He, however, bases his position of the process whereby the Oedipus complex wanes on the death instinct. Thus he concludes that each step away from the parent represents an act of parricide. This differs from the developmental point of view which takes into account selective identification and the transfer of functions of the object representations to the self representation—processes of internalization which do not destroy the object representations. This is the opposite of parricide. Each step away from the parent representations takes an aspect of those representations along in the sense that their functions are transferred, while the representations per se remain.

It has also been insufficiently considered that the object representation is not destroyed in toto by decathexis of the sexual wish. An important aspect of resolution of the oedipal conflict, therefore, is desexualization of the object relationship with the parent. This is a far cry from destruction.

The Oedipus complex wanes after the first round, only to wax again in subsequent developmental phases. At each adult developmental phase there is internalization of new, nonincestuous object representations, which promotes advancement away from primary object representations. Thus the scope and influence of the primary object representations diminish. This process, begun in childhood, continues and even escalates. By adulthood need for the primary object has receded. The parricidal ideation of childhood, an aspect of primary object need, atrophies. Establishment of new libidinal connections at adult levels now satisfies object need.

CHAPTER 12

DIAGNOSIS

W E NEED TO remind ourselves every now and then that Freud's
first discoveries were based on his self-analysis, including analysis of his own dreams. One may speculate with considerable certainty
that this led him to devote his life's work to understanding the neurotic,
structured personality. This historical fact accounts also for the elaboration of the psychoanalytic theory of neurosis by Freud's pupils to the
relative neglect of understanding the understructured personalities. Not
until long after Freud's death did exploration of the nature of these
pathologies begin in earnest (Knight 1954; Kernberg 1967, 1968).

The many reconsiderations in the literature of Freud's five cases raise
questions about whether those patients were truly structured. Schreber
was clearly psychotic, which Freud knew. It appears that the Wolf Man
was certainly understructured, which Freud overlooked because his investigations were not directed toward borderline phenomena. Whether
the Rat Man suffered from a true obsessional neurosis is also in doubt.
Similar doubts apply to Dora and to Little Hans. Today, the three latter
cases would probably be regarded as possessing both neurotic and borderline features. They would be described as having negotiated the
Fulcrum of Development toward the neurotic side in some respects,
and as having lagged in development in others, making for mixed
diagnostic pictures consisting of both structured and understructured
features.

The history of diagnosis shows that the quest for precision has led
to a search for distinct diagnostic categories into which individuals may
be cast. The concept of the person as a whole has been lost sight of
repeatedly, then rediscovered. As history repeats itself in this way, the
perspective shifts back and forth. The methodology of diagnosis has
still not arrived at a comfortable balance between the two positions.

The most recent psychiatric diagnostic scheme, *Diagnostic and Statistical Manual* (DSM-III 1980), veers in the direction of establishing explicit diagnostic criteria and away from consideration of the person as a whole. This trend repeats the early history of modern diagnosis and perhaps promises that, with time, diagnosis by symptom will once again be replaced by diagnosis of "the structure of the ego in which the symptom is embedded" (Eissler 1953).

Kraepelin introduced a method of diagnosis by outcome. If the patient recovered, he or she had suffered from the more benign manic depressive psychosis; if recovery did not take place, the illness had been and remained dementia praecox. This method has more value than appears. It is used to this very day in the practice of medicine. An infection, for example, may be treated by administration of an antibiotic. If cure takes place, the infecting agent was a bacterium, while if the illness does not yield, the presumptive infecting agent is a virus.

This applies in psychopharmacology as well. If a depression yields to lithium, the illness is manic depressive psychosis, whereas other kinds of depression have to be treated by psychotherapy where possible and alleviated (not cured) by medications other than lithium.

Kraepelin's "outcome" theory has a certain persuasive quality for an ego psychologist. We would think that if recovery takes place there is a capacity to recover or, as we (1979) have put it, a capacity for reorganization. There is, after all, no sure way to diagnose the capacity for reorganization in advance of treatment except by the relatively unreliable search for whether reorganization had ever taken place in the past history of the individual. It remains correct to maintain along with Kraepelin that the structure that recovers must be different from the structure that fails to recover.

Bleuler altered the Kraeplinian approach by changing the perspective. Psychiatric diagnosis, now, is mainly concerned with symptomatology, although contemporary elaborations of that basic procedure have carried it into rather precise areas that were unknown to Bleuler. Thus the *Diagnostic and Statistical Manual of Mental Disorders* has undergone two revisions. The third version, in current use, attempts to diagnose along three axes so that there will be interjudgment among diagnostic criteria. The scheme is atheoretical, presumably for the purpose of lending itself to universal use. The diagnostician simply looks at the symptom picture and arrives at a decision based entirely upon that assessment.

This is very different from psychoanalytic diagnosis, where the structure rather than the symptom picture is the center of the diagnostic investigation. Psychoanalysts are particularly interested in the relationship among the three agencies of structure, the relative strength of each, the nature of the conflict, how the ego deals with anxiety. The symptoms are secondary. In fact, as Rangell notes, hysterical symptoms, the very bedrock of Freud's discoveries, can exist in all levels of structuralization, proving undeniably how unreliable is diagnosis by symptom. Heretofore, conversion symptoms were believed to be certain signs of hysteria, and phobias were believed to be indicative of anxiety neurosis. Now we find those symptoms in psychosis and in borderline conditions more frequently than in neurosis. Many neuroses seen these days are relatively asymptomatic. If they were to be diagnosed by symptom, the pathology would be missed because it exists only in the character.

The psychiatric method of diagnosis appears even more radically different from the psychoanalytic when the ego psychological dimension is added. In that kind of diagnostic approach, not only is structure examined, but whether and how much structuralization has taken place is a central consideration. This is a process that must be carried out, not as separate and preliminary, but within the therapeutic situation proper. Only in that context can the transferential aspects, which reveal the level of object relations, be included in the diagnostic exploration. In such a long-term diagnostic process, the ongoing unfolding of diagnostic information inevitably becomes intertwined with treatment. In the very process of diagnosing, the patient gets better and the diagnosis changes.

This appears paradoxical. How can a firm diagnosis be made under such changing conditions? The ego psychological psychoanalyst gropes, but not in the dark. He or she determines the structure toward the outset of treatment. If the patient is structured, regressive features are dealt with as defense. The ego is assumed to be competent and treatment is directed toward working out the conflict on the oedipal level.

If we are dealing with an understructured personality, treatment is directed toward building structure in the expectation that then the ego will become competent enough to deal with oedipal conflict. In the first instance, regressive features tend to disappear as their defensive nature is understood and interpreted. In the second instance, the structure strengthens. This is what we mean by altering the diagnosis as treatment proceeds—not that we change our diagnostic minds, but that the very purpose of treatment is to alter the diagnosis for the better. Ideally, the cured neurotic would be discharged with a diagnosis of "normal." This is not possible because, as Freud pointed out in *Analysis Terminable and Interminable* (1937), not all conflict comes to the fore during the analytic time frame.

To conceive of diagnosis as a process is to accept that diagnostic information emerges slowly and only when treatment has already begun (A. Freud, H. Nagera & W. E. Freud 1965).

Therapists and analysts who are attuned to transference phenomena are aware that transference exists even before the patient's first arrival in the consultation room, in fantasies about the therapist which represent an attempt to fit him or her into the already extant object representation "slot." The speculations, musings, assumptions, and fantasies that are elaborated, consciously and unconsciously, before the first meeting with the therapist may be described as the purest form of transference, based solely upon the patient's prior object experiences, as yet unmodified by the visual appearance of the therapist, his or her mannerisms, facial expressions, assumed or actual attitudes, office setting, attire, and other "contaminants" of reality.

The initial diagnostic task is, of course, to listen to the patient's complaint and history, making the usual inferences about structure, defense, and adaptation, and eliciting unconscious fantasy and dreams where appropriate. One also thinks about the manner in which the patient deals with the therapist and what this reveals about the level and quality of the object relations. We have said that the level of object relations is the instrument of immediate contact with another person. A diagnostician attuned to developmental vicissitudes can hear reflections of developmental attainments and failures. Most important, the diagnostician-therapist can also evaluate the nature of the "slot" and especially how flexible it is. Can it alter with reality largely, slightly, or not at all? To state this in another way, the patient's approach pattern is an indicator of the object relations level and pattern.

That description of the diagnostic process suggests also that diagnostician and therapist are the same person. Such a desirable state of affairs is possible mainly in a private practice setting. In institutionalized outpatient settings there is often an "intake" person who makes the initial diagnosis before the case is assigned to a therapist. This may be a necessary evil for administrative purposes. In some settings the therapist is assigned to "intake" on a rotating basis so that she or he can continue with treatment.

Our statement about the approach behavior has to be qualified. If the approach is with excessive anxiety, that may represent a temporary regression which will right itself when the initial fears about the therapeutic encounter diminish. However, this is not to be passed over in the diagnostician's mind. It still tells us something about the patient's approach behavior. The inquiry would then have to follow the route of exploring why the object expectation is a fear-laden one. Or defense may take the opposite form—flight forward rather than regression. In that instance the patient is presenting himself or herself at a level that cannot be sustained, and, like the needle on a compass, the true level of object relations will come to rest sometime later. That way of presenting oneself is usually indicative of an adaptive attempt to connect at a higher level even though the concomitant ability to sustain it is lacking. Such patients have looked at reality and have become aware that that higher level exists; they try to live up to it. Other patients do not know that, usually because the parents did not function at that higher level. As we sometimes find ourselves saying in our case seminars, the entire family was in the playpen together. We mean that, while the developing child can only be at the level of object relations appropriate to his or her age and general developmental level, the most desirable growth-promoting medium is one in which the parents have attained self and object constancy.

Here is an illustration of how an aspect of the larger diagnostic picture can be detected and worked with in a given session:

A forty-year-old man wants the therapist to be an omnipotent partner who gets him everything he wants. He has been married and divorced twice. His current woman friend has gone abroad to be with her adolescent children for the Christmas holidays. "I want her to spend Christmas with me," he roars at the therapist. When he gets no response he roars even louder, "You're supposed to help me get her to do what I want." When this does not succeed he slumps down in his chair and loses interest in the remainder of the session.

Obviously, the threshold of frustration is low, but that is the lesser problem. The greater one is that the therapist loses value if he does not comply with the patient's wishes. This is at wide variance from object constancy. Also prominent is the failure of reality testing, since there is no way that the therapist can force his friend to remain with him for Christmas even if there could be some therapeutic rationale for making such an attempt. The patient withdraws into his narcissistic fantasies where his objects-as-part-of-the-self do not oppose him.

Therapy has taken place in the very process of diagnosing this segment of the patient's problem; the therapist has not put himself at the patient's disposal. Every therapist would follow this apparently simple procedure, except perhaps those who believe that something is to be gained by joining in with the patient's unrealistic demand. But what has been accomplished by the stance that this therapist did adopt? Bearing in mind that object connection is always paramount, the patient has to contend with the frustration in order to retain the object in some tenuous way. Although he withdraws, he does not leave treatment. He enters into a narcissistic arrangement such as we have described (1979). The therapist has made a move by not complying.

Now diagnosis alternates with treatment. The therapist has to wait to see whether the narcissistic shell can be penetrated. The next move will be up to the patient who will, sooner or later, offer another opening. The therapist will, of course, be alert to it. But more than that, he will be alert to small mutations. Will the patient continue to make the same unrealistic demand? Will the demands alter with reality? Will the frustration promote more adaptive mechanisms than withdrawal from the real object world? If that should happen, the therapist must be there with immediate and unflagging support of this new growth level, not with praise but with readiness to meet it in the hope that, as an object in the real world, he can compete ever so slightly with the objects in the fantasy world. Let us construct an ongoing dialogue:

PATIENT: You haven't responded to anything I've said.
THERAPIST: When you withdrew like that I thought you didn't want me to.
PATIENT: I see now that that does happen, and I suppose that when I get frustrated I do withdraw, but then I come out of it.
THERAPIST: Well, that tells me that you are here with me now.
PATIENT: Yes, it gets lonely there.
THERAPIST: I can only be with you when you seek me out.

This dialogue describes emergence from the narcissistic arrangement. It is expected that it will be temporary. There will be many forays back and forth before the comfort of an object relationship in reality can gain a competitive edge over the comfort of the world that can be arranged to one's liking. Also described is the manner in which the therapist implies that it is the patient's task to extract from the environment—in this instance from the therapeutic situation. In chapter 1 we discussed promotion of the division of labor between patient and therapist. Here we illustrate one of the many ways in which this may be accomplished. It must always be at the patient's behest, when he or she experiences the need. If the therapist reaches out before then, it appears to the patient to be the therapist's need.

To discuss this clinical illustration in the framework of the overall problem of diagnosis, we must address the tendency to apply diagnostic "labels." This may be ascribed to an interest in precision and predictability. There is a certain security in the description of pathology in entities. Thus, a patient such as the one above could be diagnosed as narcissistic (Kohut), as suffering from a narcissistic personality disorder (Kernberg), or as understructured with a narcissistic arrangement (Blanck & Blanck 1979). We believe that our position offers flexibility. It states the patient's position accurately as narcissistic, yet it leaves room for consideration of the totality of structure, for the person-as-a-whole, rather than focusing on the segment of pathology, outstanding as that is, for the pathology is not analogous to a tumor that exists in an otherwise healthy body. When all fourteen points on the Fulcrum of Development are taken into account, it will probably be shown that the preponderance of diagnostic criteria pivot to the understructured side. In the process of curing the narcissistic arrangement, alterations in those other aspects of structuralization will change in conjunction with therapeutic attention to the narcissistic feature. To mention only the most obvious one here, frustration tolerance will stretch. This is accomplished not simply by frustrating the patient and allowing him to stew, but by being at his side to lend support while he endures the frustration. This is not an innovation in technique. We emphasize the object relations feature—that frustration is more tolerable in the presence of an attuned object.

The authors of the *Diagnostic and Statistical Manual* recognize that persons with the same symptomatology and even the same mental disorder are not necessarily alike. But the purpose for which DSM-III was introduced was to improve upon DSM-II, which did not provide interjudge reliability, not to improve upon the fundamental diagnostic philosophy. The DSM-III proposes five axes, the first three of which constitute the official diagnosis. To arrive at the diagnosis *borderline,* for example, there would be five out of seven forms of characteristic manifestations of that disorder. But where is the *person* who displays those manifestations? The following highlights that important factor of diagnosis:

> A patient seeks therapy with the presenting problem of impotence. He is in his forties, has not married because of his problem, but enjoys great social success despite it because of his attractive appearance and social skills. He functions, for the most part, on a realistic object relations level and is therefore able to command considerable respect in his position as an executive in a large corporation. Organic cause for his symptom has been ruled out. He is potent for masturbatory purposes, which are accompanied by heterosexual fantasies, but he cannot function in a heterosexual situation in reality. There have been no homosexual contacts.

At superficial glance, the presumptive psychoanalytic diagnosis, if based on symptoms alone, would be a neurosis with severe castration anxiety. If diagnosis is made according to the DSM-III scheme, one would refer to the statement that "the essential feature [in impotence] is inhibition in the appetitive or psychophysiological changes that characterize the complete sexual response" (p. 275). The principal diagnosis would be *inhibited sexual excitement,* coded 302.72. Quite properly, the manual refers to issues of differential diagnosis, such as whether disturbance in sexual function antedates depression or whether it is secondary to it. Room is left also for personality disorders, marital discord, and other interpersonal problems which may have a bearing on the diagnosis. In the case we are considering here, a secondary diagnosis according to DSM-III would be *borderline personality disorder,* code number 301.82. The first diagnosis stresses the symptomatology and behavior, while the second suggests consideration of the total personality. In either case, the clinician is provided with no clue as to etiology and, since DSM-III is atheoretical, with no guide to treatment.

Continuing our clinical presentation:

> The therapist did not think analysis to be the treatment of choice because there appeared to be certain features of understructuralization. There was especially question about the object relations level because the patient's life-style was essentially an isolated one. The patient was told that a schedule of three sessions per week would offer optimal therapeutic opportunity. However, the therapist had only two sessions immediately available, with the expectation that a third session would open up shortly. The patient balked at the time slot. His rationalization was that the time offered would bring him to his office one half hour later than usual on the mornings of his sessions. Taking into account that executives on his level are not required to work regular hours and often remain at the office late in the day, as well as working at home evenings and weekends, he made an uneasy peace with the two sessions that were available. When the third session opened up he went into a panic about arriving late at work yet another morning.
>
> The triviality of the manifest material for a while obscured the extent of the anxiety and consequent regression. But it began to become clear that he was unable to deal with this external matter because the structure was less competent than it appeared at first. Although the therapist had begun cautiously enough by not undertaking analysis immediately, he was surprised at the extent of the collapse.
>
> The patient did not dare oppose the therapist by refusing the third

session, nor could he face the possibility of being questioned by his superior officer if he were to arrive late. This despite his acknowledgment that the likelihood of being questioned was nil. Nevertheless, he became unable to function to a degree that threatened his job. He failed to meet deadlines and to perform on the level that the company had reason to expect of him. He also began to come late for his therapy sessions. We have suggested (1979) that lateness in the understructured personality represents something different from the resistance of the structured patient. In this case, as in many, it appeared to be an attempt to deal with anxiety by action because the defensive system was too primitive. To put this another way, the defensive function of the ego is inoperative because structuralization has not reached the point where the ego is competent enough to employ signal anxiety and defense mechanisms.

The patient said he felt numb. After much exploration this, too, turned out to represent a primitive defense of the fight or flight type; in this instance it was an almost total withdrawal in the face of extreme danger. The therapist began to connect the impotence with the withdrawal, and realized that the anxiety was not limited to castration but more resembled the totality of fear of annihilation.

Understanding this regressive floor made the peculiar work history more understandable, too. This patient had been dismissed from four or more high-level jobs after promising starts. In the initial exploratory sessions he attributed this to corporate politics. While that probably always plays a part, the pattern of his promising beginning and swift panic shortly thereafter was becoming evident. It applied to his professional functioning, to his sexual functioning, and to his behavior in the transference. Although aware of these retreats, the patient, having had therapy before, described them in neurotic-like terms. "I begin to drag my feet, or dig in my heels." These phrases hardly did justice to the enormity of the inaction.

The therapist realized that the patient could not easily resolve the dilemma that revolved around undertaking a third session even though it had been agreed upon at the outset. At this level of anxiety it threatened to be damaging to pursue it. The patient was told that he needed more time to decide this issue and that, in the interim, the therapist would fill the time. His relief was instantaneous and vast. He recovered some of the regressive loss of function, but not all.

The therapist learned still more. Not only was the patient's work

situation in disarray, his apartment was a shambles as well. He revealed how shabbily he was living, although in a good neighborhood.
He had not much more than a bed for furniture, no chairs. He hoped
that he would make his apartment more comfortable some day, and
he even fantasied that he might be able to entertain a woman there.

The first impression—that there was better structuralization, although not quite on a neurotic level—had to be revised downward
because of the inability of the ego to control the regression. The regressive floor was too low for easy recoverability; regression was not in
the service of the ego (Kris 1952). This single feature is one of several
that sharply distinguishes the better-structured from the less adequately
structured personalities. This alteration in diagnosis illustrates the continuous process of ever-modifying diagnostic thinking, free of the con-
straint of strict categorization.

The following case was presented by a student therapist:

> A thirty-eight-year-old woman, wife of a prominent member of
> the community, was arrested for shoplifting. Because of the husband's
> position, the judge put her on probation with the proviso that she
> have treatment. The student therapist was deeply concerned because,
> in the fourth session, the patient began to negate the treatment, to
> accuse the therapist of only wanting her money. She considered dis-
> continuing despite the court order, and to all of the therapist's at-
> tempts to get at the underlying reason for her "resistance," she
> maintained that she had nothing to say.
>
> The history that was taken was meager because the therapist was
> eager to secure the case and therefore did not wish to spend time on
> history taking. This is sometimes a valid way to begin, especially
> with nonvoluntary patients. This one came by court order; others
> come because the school wishes it, because the spouse insists, or for
> other coercive reasons. The problem in such instances is that the
> patient is not yet a patient in his or her own right.
>
> About this patient we know only that she grew up in a small
> town. She was an only child because there had been three infant
> deaths before she was born. She was cherished and overprotected to
> the point of being prevented from engaging in ordinary childhood
> activities. She married at eighteen.
>
> She moved with her husband to another city. They remained child-

less. She busied herself with volunteer work which she detailed to the therapist in the first three sessions. The therapist reported feeling bored. Boredom as a countertransference can sometimes be useful in informing the therapist that this is the patient's unconscious intent. Armed with this knowledge, one can engage in exploration of why the patient wants the therapist to be lulled. In this instance, however, this was not so. The therapist acknowledged to the supervisor that she was bored because of her own depreciation of volunteer work and her lack of interest in the details.

Supervisors are often obliged to deal with whatever information is presented, no matter how sparse, in order to enable the therapist to help the patient. This involves supporting the therapist's efforts as well as lending oneself to the needs of the patient. A chastened therapist is not likely to approach the patient comfortably. Timing in supervision is as important, in its own way, as is timing of interventions in the treatment process. When the case is well secured there will be time to teach the therapist how she might have begun the case in a more useful way.

What is timely now is to form a tentative diagnostic picture that will give the therapist a frame of reference within which to proceed. It has to be strongly emphasized, because we are surmising on the basis of such meager information, that any corrective details that are elicited can alter the diagnostic impression in one direction or another.

The first assumption is that the patient's mother was anxious about the child's physical survival and that autonomous functioning was not uppermost in her mind. We can also assume, in this vein, that the practicing subphase was fraught with interpersonal conflict between a child who wanted to venture and a mother who needed to protect. So we think of this woman as having ventured despite the mother's anxiety, but at the price of the object connection. The "boring" details of her volunteer work are to be regarded as the manifest level. She is saying that she is competent and can function. Seen in this light, her "resistance" represents her conflict—fear of losing her dearly won independence the moment she finds herself in a situation of needing help. She has nothing to say. The therapist only wants her money. This puts them at more than arm's length.

In this case, then, one keeps in mind the presenting symptom of having taken something, the fact that this is not yet a voluntary patient, and her approach behavior which represents a conflict between deep need for the object and fear of loss of autonomy. Let us look at some dialogue from the fifth session, when the therapist has had the benefit of supervisory help:

PATIENT: I have nothing to say.
THERAPIST: It's hard for you to be here. (It is premature to say, "You are frightened to be here." That would be correct in content but incorrent in timing because the patient is defended against her anxiety. If we interfere with the defense she will be overwhelmed.)
PATIENT: I can do hard things. I work hard for the hospital.

The response is oblique. The emphasis continues to be on functioning. The need for the object must be defended against. As we see this as the adaptive mode of maintaining autonomy, it takes on a less pejorative connotation. Without it the patient would succumb to merger at some subphase level and lose her capacity to function. It is, nevertheless, valid to regard it as resistance as well, and that, of course, is diagnostically useful. The place where resistance is employed shows where the conflict exists, where anxiety becomes palpable.

THERAPIST: Your hospital work is important to you. We can continue to talk about that, but also your reason for being here tells us that something was troubling you when you took the scarf from the store.

Here the therapist goes along with the patient, but not altogether, reminding her that the solution of volunteer work is a compromise that does not always allay her anxiety, that she shoplifted in a moment of intense need that crept through the defense. This cannot be stated to the patient in that form; it is embedded in the therapist's phrasing of the intervention.

Our very speculative diagnostic thinking shows this patient poised between her need for autonomy and her need for the object. The superordinate ego had no opportunity to bring the conflict to resolution in the orderly process of organizing her development, as would have been possible in a more growth-promoting mother-child experience. Also to be noted is that the aggressive drive, when seen as powering the developmental thrust, has brought this woman to a position more favorable than nonconflictual surrender to the symbiotic closeness. Although she cannot move out of it, she strains to do so. The prognosis is favorable; she can succeed with therapeutic help.

The student therapist has to be instructed to tolerate the boredom for the sake of joining the patient where she can be reached. This means becoming interested in the hospital work, not for its manifest content, but because it supports functioning and does not expose the regressive wish before the patient can bear to know it. One can predict that, by meeting her on her own ground and yet leading her a step beyond, as illustrated, the object need will intensify and another crisis will ensue. But then it will be within the context of the therapeutic relationship and therefore may not have to be acted out in a symbolic act like shoplifting. The therapist buys time in order for the therapy to become the very environment within which the conflict can be contained.

It is so often said that diagnosis and treatment proceed side by side that it seems trite to repeat that here. Yet it bears augmentation. In every patient session we are forming diagnostic impressions and tailoring the short-range intervention so that it will have both the immediate effect and also contribute to the long-range goal.

CHAPTER 13
TECHNICAL IMPLICATIONS:
INTRODUCTION

THE CONCEPT of a superordinate ego does not dictate radically new treatment techniques. Rather, it strongly affirms already established guidelines for the psychoanalytic therapeutic process. It alters the perspective, thereby offering greater potential for understanding the patient. Technical precepts that have been known for some time are understood in greater depth. A platform for further research is provided. In its essence our proposal of a superordinate ego is no more than another elaboration of the structural theory. It advances the well-known extensions by Anna Freud and by Hartmann.

Each of the important areas of technique is reconsidered here in a way that reemphasizes or extends that which is already known about it. We have discussed transference (chapter 8) and diagnosis (chapter 12). Chapter 14 will deal with interpretation and working through; chapter 15 will discuss evenly suspended attention and tracking the patient's associations; chapter 16 will deal with the process of termination.

Here we review our earlier writings on technique. We then discuss topography and structure; modifications in the technique of uncovering; the benign climate and the therapeutic alliance. As has been our policy, we do not attempt to present a comprehensive review of every aspect of technique, but focus on those to which we can add a few new thoughts. We begin with the reiteration of the centrality of object relations.

Spitz's insight into early mentation affirms the validity of Freud's several definitions of identification. The first of these, that an emotional tie exists before object cathexis, links with the later ones—the intermediate definition that identification replaces a lost object tie, and the later definition of identification as a normal process of internalization. All three definitions contain the common denominator that the human being is influenced by his or her caretaking objects. What is clearly implied are that this influence has a decisive effect upon one's perception of the world, that we are "rational" only up to a point, and that perception of reality is first evoked out of the relationship with the primary object. The need for object connection continues to influence and sometimes to distort reality testing throughout life and, as we have described, accounts for the phenomenon of transference.

The discovery that input is received and processed from the first day of life forces us to consider that coherent organization of that material must begin at once in order to establish and maintain equilibrium of the total organism. Each new experience must be forced into place within the community of the whole. Differentiation and integration proceed simultaneously. The findings of the infant researchers inform also:

1. that object relations are the internalized result of interaction with the primary object;
2. that, therefore, the primary object plays a basic role in psychic structuring;
3. that the infant brings his or her innate endowment to bear upon the interaction; and
4. that, in fact, the interaction does not consist of an equal partnership; the role of the infant in adaptation to the environment and to the dyadic interaction is the greater one.

In extrapolating these discoveries to technique, the therapist is brought to appreciate ever more strongly that therapeutic address is to the whole person. In a sense this merely restates Anna Freud's (1936) proposal that psychoanalytic treatment must address not only the id, but the ego and superego as well. That, at the time, took technique a long step toward consideration of the whole person rather than consideration of the vicissitudes of the drives alone. This inclusive approach imposes greater demand upon the therapist:

1. To understand the developmental processes of the component

parts in order to grasp the logic of the way in which the whole is functioning; especially to understand the nature of development during critical periods (Spitz) in order to properly evaluate where maturation and development have succeeded and where they have failed to come together.
2. To develop a flexibly attuned diagnostic eye and ear. This is the antithesis of attempts to locate the patient in "exact" diagnostic pigeonholes.
3. To diminish reliance upon form and to maintain a precise definition of ego boundaries.
4. To maintain the therapeutic alliance and to exploit the therapeutic differential in the patient's interest.
5. To tolerate uncertainty. If the patient does not and cannot know all there is about himself and his experiences, then surely the therapist can only grope toward better understanding, with the patient's active cooperation.

Review of Our Technical Proposals

In our 1974 volume we distinguished between psychoanalysis and psychotherapy. There was still much doubt that some of the techniques of psychoanalysis could be useful in psychotherapy. Authors on the technique of psychotherapy who preceded us were of the opinion that transference was to be avoided in psychotherapy (Tarachow 1963; Murphy 1965). But we noted that transference does occur despite attempts to avoid and to overlook it; and we believed that it can and should be used. This, after all, merely parallels Freud's original discovery of the usefulness of transference in psychoanalysis. Since it exists, it is essential to use it by giving it the right turn; to ignore it is detrimental to the treatment.

We also described, particularly in the case of Mr. Baker, how psychotherapy can proceed to become psychoanalysis as the structure is strengthened. We would modify that now for a certain segment of the patient population by reducing the very sharp distinction we made between the two treatment modalities. To be specific, we have found that there is a large patient population that has long been described, by those who prefer to use distinct diagnostic statements, as neurotic with borderline features, or borderline with neurotic features. These patients possess a modicum of structure and therefore are involved in some intersystemic conflict, yet at the same time are at levels of object relations and possess certain ego weaknesses that require ego-building measures. Technique, in such instances, demands the utmost versatility and flexibility on the part of the therapist, who must be able to move from a more psychotherapeutic (ego-building) approach to a more psychoanalytic (interpretative) stance, and back again, as the material dictates.

We also began to think, in 1974, that the totality of the organization of the psyche is far more important an indicator of how development has proceeded than are the individual symptoms. This, of course, merely means that our diagnostic thinking proceeded along developmental lines. We developed this thought more fully in 1979, when we began to view ego as the very process of organization. Paraphrasing Hartmann, and modifying his thought only slightly, we proposed that the ego is defined by its function*ing*. We therefore elaborated ego-building techniques designed to advance the organizing process. We paid specific attention to the identification of malformations in organization and, prognostically, to the evaluation of the capacity for reorganization. We also addressed problems of differential diagnosis, such as the distinction between the search for replication of early (inadequate) object experience, and transference (a difficult matter that we believe we have now made more precise in chapter 8 of this volume). We discussed techniques for the enhancement of self-esteem, for the promotion of affect differentiation, for aiding self-soothing, and for the promotion of the separation-individuation process.

Here our thinking advances as we are led to consider that the organizing process takes place on two levels: the level of organization of daily experiences which we have termed *programs,* involving specific ego functions; and the level at which the individual functions are integrated into the more or less coherent functioning of the whole, the superordinate level.

Topography and Structure

The concept of the superordinate ego does not deviate from the structural theory as proposed by Freud. We posit that there are both an ego in the narrow sense of immediate functioning and a *super* ego in the broader sense as the guardian of the overall structure. Were it not for the fact that the term *superego* is preempted, that term would suffice to apply to what we designate as superordinate ego.

The features that distinguish psychoanalytic theory from all other psychologies are: that there is an unconscious and therefore there are unconscious fantasy and unconscious conflict; and that processes of internalization lead to structuralization.

The discovery of the topography of the psyche which Freud came upon at the turn of the twentieth century in itself set psychoanalysis apart from academic psychology and from psychiatry. Yet, by 1923, the topographic theory appeared to Freud to be too primitive to explain the phenomena he was observing clinically. It proposed simply that the id is unconscious and that the ego is conscious. It took Freud those many years to realize, from his clinical data, that part of the ego is also unconscious, "and Heaven knows how important a part may be unconscious, undoubtedly is unconscious" (1923:18).

In addition to his thoughts about a *gesamt Ich,* which we have stressed, Freud had certain understated thoughts about technique that should be rescued from obscurity and given appropriate place alongside the technical precepts contained in his 1912–13 papers on technique. His recognition that not everything that is unconscious can be brought to the light of day restricts therapeutic zeal to realistic limits and emphasizes that there are factors that will forever remain invisible but will exert powerful influence nevertheless. How remarkable Freud's insight is into the fact that there is an unrecoverable aspect of the unconscious can only be appreciated in the light of Spitz's very much later (1965) contribution regarding coenesthetic sensing. "The mute invisible tides" that remain with us throughout life and that influence our object relations and our behavior so profoundly can never be fully known to us.

The topographic theory, as it gained in sophistication, acquired an intermediary level between conscious and unconscious, designated as *preconscious.* It is the preconscious level of the psyche that plays such an important role in technique because material from the unconscious has to be "lifted" to the preconscious in order for it to become interpretable.

As we have shown, Arlow and Brenner (1964) try to simplify matters by their contention that the structural theory is superior to and therefore supersedes the topographic. This oversimplifies without offering a solution by integration. It is generally acknowledged that the structural theory has taken psychoanalytic theory construction a giant step. In fact, ego psychology could not have evolved without it, for it is the very foundation upon which ego psychology is built. Yet we still have to account for how material moves from one level of consciousness to another—that is to say, we still need a topographic theory as well as a theory of structure.

Uncovering

Freud states quite clearly in 1923, "We recognize that the *Ucs.* does not coincide with the repressed; it is still true that all that is repressed is *Ucs.*, but not all that is *Ucs.* is repressed" (p. 18). Analysts had to reason out for themselves again and again that it was the very discovery that part of the ego is unconscious that led Freud to the structural theory, that id and unconscious are no longer to be regarded as synonymous, that the id is unconscious but it is not *the* unconscious.

The confusion is not simply semantic. Here may also lie the historical roots of the confusion between drive and affect that persists today. The id, all agree, is the repository of the drives. But few pause to reason that, since the drives can only be known through their derivatives, libido and aggression cannot be manifest.

Many more examples may be found in the psychoanalytic literature to illustrate how hard tradition dies. Another one, as we showed in chapter 11, is that the terms *preoedipal* and *pregenital* are still confused because of the historical fact that the theory of psychosexual maturation was proposed long before a theory of object relations. Analysts who remain more familiar with psychosexuality find it difficult to distinguish between that line of development and the object relations line.

After Anna Freud's demonstration that equal technical consideration is to be given to the ego and to the drives, the next step awaited Kris, who showed, some twenty years later, that the principal analytic purpose is not to uncover repressed memories but to unravel the patterns that the organizing process weaves in the ongoing march of development. In effect this shifts the focus from uncovering per se toward ego functioning. Uncovering is not eliminated, but now occupies a secondary, auxiliary position.

Hartmann (1951) pointed out that technique inevitably lags behind theory. Kris' contribution in the area of the theory of technique highlighted the analytic objectives that transcend simple uncovering. But, because of the lag, it is difficult to root out the idea that the very essence of psychoanalytic technique is to uncover. Based upon the deeply ingrained conviction implanted by the earliest theories of hysteria—that neurosis is the consequence of repression—the analyst is taught to pursue the unconscious vigorously, to deal with the resistances for the very purpose of bringing repressed material into the preconscious where it can be interpreted.

Yet, as we have come to understand preoedipal life, an entirely new dimension is added to the analytic process. While repressed conflict around oedipal wishes remains the core of neurotic formations, the preoedipal experiences that determine the shaping of the Oedipus complex now influence our technique in most cases, for few if any have the good fortune to have experienced smooth preoedipal development. Where preoedipal experience has been more rather than less favorable, traditional analytic methods might suffice, precisely because the thrust of ego-organizing processes results in a structure on the superordinate level, capable of responding to classical psychoanalytic techniques. Where, however, preoedipal difficulties have seriously distorted the shape of the oedipal formation, the consequences of those experiences have to be dealt with by other technical means.

One would wish that early issues would present themselves first in the treatment of adult pathology. This is an impossible ideal. The reality is that organization proceeds despite developmental inadequacies; therefore, systematic ordering of the material is rarely, if ever, possible. The analyst may find it desirable to defer some issues and attempts to do so when this can be effected. More often, the material appears in chaotic form and can be ordered only slightly. Where ordering is possible, the consequences of preoedipal distortions in object relations take priority in the expectation that, later, the patient will be better positioned for coping with oedipal conflict. This, as is clear by now, is because distortions on the oedipal level of self and object relations are caused by the persistence of deficits that precede it. More often than was before realized, reflections of malformations on oedipal and preoedipal levels appear in condensed form as the final product of the ongoing organizing process.

The following case illustrates extreme pathology in object relations, a narcissistic arrangement that includes a distorted oedipal position within the totality of malformed organization. The oedipal issue could not be avoided despite the analyst's knowledge that the structure was not competent enough to deal with it by uncovering. The analyst would not have directed his efforts actively toward uncovering, but oedipal material appeared nevertheless.

> This understructured patient had had a psychotic mother who had been unable to constitute a bridge to reality for the child. The patient, as an adult, demonstrated that his considerable talent and capacity for adaptation had enabled him to compensate for this gap. As with most childhood adaptations to unmet developmental needs, it became maladaptive later. He went through life trying to test reality alone, without confirmation. Often he was mistaken in his judgments. Always he lived with uncertainty. He had adopted an "I have to go it alone" attitude that expects nothing from the other person. Such patients do not realize that something is missing in the interaction; they believe that life is that way. We described earlier how it is more difficult to detect *what was not* than *what was*.
>
> The deficits in self and object relations came to light in the transference as the analyst realized that the patient was not turning to him for confirmation of observations about which the patient held considerable uncertainty. The analyst commented upon this many times until the patient became aware that he was constantly working to fill in gaps alone because there was no expectation that he would be joined in those efforts.

This in no way advocates that the analyst or therapist actively provide or compensate for missed experiences. In most instances short of psychosis, it is only necessary to detect those "empty spaces," and to point to the impoverished object expectation whenever it appears. This is to broaden the patient's purview and to expand object expectation. It does not follow that, because the primary object had not been able to perform the needed function at the phase-specific time, belated performance by the therapist will be reparative.

Because this is one of the most misunderstood areas of the extrapolation of ego psychological theory to technique, we find it necessary to stress repeatedly that reparenting has little or no place in the treatment of adult pathology because, by the time the patient has become an adult, the deficiency in early object relations has been compensated for. Often, but far from always, compensation takes the form of a narcissistic arrangement as we described in 1979.

This patient was unprepared to deal with oedipal issues because, in the absence of supportive object representations, such persons cannot conceive that the parent of the same sex will see him through in the oedipal crisis any more than either parent had seen him through earlier developmental issues. Absent was the necessary representation of an object who is oriented in reality, who stands by and supports.

That he filled the gap for himself made real object relationships difficult. He experienced a vague need for other persons without knowledge of what another person is for. This was a permeable narcissistic arrangement. The patient had not withdrawn from object negotiation altogether. He needed others, but lacked the expectation that support and confirmation can be functions of the object. Because of the permeability he was available for "interpretation" of this fact. This is not interpretation in the traditional sense of verbalizing material that had first been lifted from unconscious to preconscious.

Oedipal material appeared from time to time, especially in dreams. The oedipal configuration lacked object representations that would facilitate entry into the oedipal position proper. Normally, the father is the feared rival as well as the loving escort who had already served to escort the child through earlier developmental crises. The normal maternal representation would include assurance, out of competent contact with reality, that the incest taboo would be maintained.

As oedipal issues appeared in the patient's dreams, they were acknowledged but not fully interpreted. The analyst had to work with repair of the object expectation, while supporting the distress the patient felt when he understood his oedipal wish in the midst of feeling so alone in attempting to cope with it.

This illustrates that there can indeed be conflict in an understructured personality and that its appearance cannot always be avoided or deferred. This is especially so in the case of a knowledgeable patient who has oedipal dreams and would be made more anxious if the analyst were to avoid them. One deals with them, understanding that the very shape of the conflict is different from that of the more familiar structured conflict. Although the material appears, it is not because the treatment has had the purpose of uncovering. The principal therapeutic task is not to uncover but to build more confident object expectation. When that is accomplished, the oedipal conflict will become manageable in a more productive way.

The Benign Climate

The term *benign climate* is generally understood as it refers to the more obvious of the therapist's responsibilities. These are:

1. Provision of a comfortable physical environment in which the therapy is conducted.
2. Reliability with regard to regularity of appointments.
3. Use of the sessions solely in the interest of the patient.
4. Neutrality and absence of value judgment.
5. Acceptance of both criticism and praise without narcissistic affront or gratification.

Because the word *benign* is sometimes interpreted to mean undemanding or even overindulgent, we are obliged to emphasize that imposition of optimal (growth promoting) frustration is a most important feature of the benign climate. Overindulgence and overpermissiveness, failure to intervene appropriately lest the patient become anxious, are countertransference problems that call for personal examination on the part of the therapist.

Now we introduce a qualitative elaboration of the concept of the benign climate which so alters its generally accepted meaning as to call for a new term. But, because we believe that random introduction of new terms tends to confuse more than to clarify, we prefer to describe rather than label our elaboration.

We describe a delicate but precise stance on the part of the therapist that is designed to repair deficiencies in object relations. There are in the literature several terms that approach but do not go fully to the heart of this matter. These are: tact, benign climate, neutrality, evenly suspended attention, therapeutic alliance, attunement, empathy, holding environment, safety feeling. None of these (and even all taken together) encompasses the quality of the object relationship that must prevail in order for the patient to feel fully understood in the affective realm. To attain that objective, we must train ourselves to listen in a new way, to hear the object relations deficit that has come about as the result of sustained developmental patterns of affective misalliance.

In *Ego Psychology II,* we referred to the therapist as an instrument. What we are suggesting now is that that instrument can be refined beyond evenly suspended attention, beyond attunement, beyond even empathy, in order to become able to detect the repetition in the therapeutic relationship of the precise deficiency in the primary object relationship. Those who advocate the concept *empathy* attempt to deal with this matter, but they tend to regard the deficiency as the consequence of parental failure. To us, that is one-sided because of our theoretical position that object relations develop out of interaction. Therefore, the phenomenon that we encounter in the therapeutic relationship is not solely the consequence of parental failure but is the *resultant* of the interaction between parent and child to which the child contributes the larger part.

The task of the therapist is to analyze (break down into component elements) this resultant to find the component to the primary interaction that was contributed by the patient. We are not likely to find the true parental component, nor do we need it. As we provide space for the patient's contribution to emerge, we can then "interpret" in the expectation that the patient will begin, slowly, to alter his or her input into the therapeutic relationship in a new form of interaction that will lead to an altered resultant. This is a process of erosion, and takes place slowly, at best.

This new dimension to the listening process imposes a new and greater demand upon the therapist because the factors that we are searching out lie in the affective realm. It alters the very definition of interpretation from that of a pronouncement across the chasm created by the diacritic mode to inclusion of whatever portion of the coenesthetic mode that remains with us as adults.

The benign climate also means that the therapist retains leadership by not yielding to the patient's poor judgment. There are patients who have not adequately developed the important ego function of judgment. Even some who are highly structured and are presumed to have developed it are swayed by affect or by unconscious fantasy in their exercise of it. We do not abandon them to their own devices. This relates to the technique for dealing with acting out. In 1974 we clarified the difference between acting and acting out. Acting, we said, is the result of direct impulse discharge. Acting out involves unconscious fantasy as the determinant of action which takes place at the expense of judgment.

We include within the definition of the benign climate consideration for the patient's affective state and for the subjective reasonableness of the patient's requests even when we deem it undesirable to go along with them. It acknowledges that the patient's goals and purposes deserve a fair hearing. The benign climate especially includes suspension of value judgment, as Sharpe illustrated when she said that if we become critical of Bottom he will refuse to disport upon the stage.

We illustrate by describing five different ways of understanding the same manifest behavior. A patient behaves in a manner that indicates that he regards the therapist as disapproving because:

1. The parent in reality was disapproving. In an understructured patient this would represent "object replication"—search for the continuation of familiar object experience based upon object need. In a structured patient this would represent the classical mistaking of the present for the past.
2. The parent was overindulgent. Here the patient needs to know where the limits lie and seeks disapproval in order to be stopped from going too far.
3. The patient is disapproving of the analyst and projects that attitude onto the analyst.
4. The patient projects his or her superego onto the analyst.

These are commonplace. Most subject to misunderstanding is a fifth possibility—that of the patient whose separation-individuation thrusts were not welcomed. Such a person would be presenting disapproved-of self-images. While this, too, may be understood as a repetition in the transference, it is quite different from the classical one. Such a patient is functioning in the experiential realm and cannot respond to a transference interpretation.

In the first instance, an interpretation (properly timed) such as "Do you now recognize that it was your father who was that way?" reduces the transference to the genetic. In the fifth instance, that would be a misaddress because the understructured patient who is living in the immediacy of the experience rather than in the structure cannot absorb an interpretation that tells him or her, in effect, that the present is being mistaken for the past, and that the transfer is from a level of object relations that appreciates that the primary object was a whole, other person. The correct technical move in that instance is attunement to the preponderance of disapproved-of self-images, to the longing to perpetuate that state of affairs in order to maintain closeness to the object-images-as-part-of-the-self-images, and to note that the need to be disapproved of is greatest when an independent thought occurs or an independent act is contemplated, for that is when object loss is feared.

The Therapeutic Alliance

The therapeutic alliance is related to attunement in the benign climate. Alliance is a joining together in a common cause. Much has been written in the texts about ways of enabling the patient to join with the analyst against the pathology, for it is recognized that, despite the patient's consciously stated desire for help, the pathology tends to seize the ego and force it to oppose the treatment. This, of course, is because the ego has the function of defense against the anxiety that the treatment threatens to evoke.

We add to these well-known technical precepts that the therapeutic alliance also involves maintenance of a relationship in which the patient continues to accept the therapist as a catalyst for growth activity. This gains specificity as we understand the derivation of less than adequate levels of object relations in the "programming" of past experience, fixed assumptions, and fixed object expectations. Thus, the therapist is able to give the resistance the "right turn" only when the therapist has helped the patient appreciate that the pathology, not the therapist, is the enemy. To accomplish this, one must shift the patient's perception that the problem is external to recognition of the internal source.

In our several discussions of the difference between the resistances of the structured personality and the similar-appearing behavior of the understructured, we have shown that a misalliance can be created by misinterpreting the behavior of the understructured patient in terms that apply to the person on a higher level. Careful differential diagnosis is called for in order to be able to realize that, in some instances, that which appears to be resistance is in fact behavior based on a lower level of development. The ego of such an individual cannot process an interpretation of resistance which would, in fact, be incorrect.

The therapeutic alliance is also furthered by the promotion of safety feeling. For the developing child, continuous safety feeling is required as the context in which optimal development takes place. For the adult patient who has not experienced such safety feeling, it accrues in the treatment situation as the patient experiences the therapist's reliability. The patient develops trust and confidence. This is much more than the well-known bedside manner of physicians of a bygone era. But the stance of the "country doctor" was not a pose or role; ideally, it reflected the character and capacity for object relations of the physician. The patient's trust must be earned in the actual interchange between patient and therapist, even if the therapist already possesses authority and value because of his or her reputation in the community.

This involves far more than a friendly demeanor. In fact, an over-friendly attitude is counterproductive and contraindicated most of the time. Some patients complain if not met with a cheerful greeting. This constitutes a necessary, temporary misalliance. But the therapist would be making an egregious error by imposing a mood or attitude that deviates from neutrality and thereby fails to leave the field free for the patient's mood. An alliance is obtained when it is appreciated that the therapist is more interested in how the patient feels than in imposing his or her own feelings.

As knowledge about heretofore unexplored facets of development increases, we gain more insight into the minute details and how to tune in to them. When scientists could only examine specimens with the naked eye, they did indeed add to our store of knowledge. With the invention of the microscope, much more came into the field of vision. The electron microscope now provides for vastly sharper scrutiny of details that were heretofore invisible. In the area of psychoanalytic observation, Mahler had only silent motion picture cameras at the time of her famous study. Modern investigators have video cameras that provide sound, color, and a sharper picture of the child's activity. As the minutiae of the developmental process become better known, they will accumulate until quantity turns into quality. Then a new organizing principle will appear within which the new information will become incorporated.

CHAPTER 14
INTERPRETATION

ONE OF the most powerful epigrams is "The truth shall set you free." Probably it is also one of the most useful, although that, of course, is impossible to measure. But it was a mainstay of Freud's early work, as he became forcefully aware of the damage caused by social hypocrisy about human sexuality. Treatment of his early cases on hysteria was based upon his conviction that when his patients "knew" the hidden truth they would be cured of their neuroses.

Interpretation has long been considered to be the prime tool of psychoanalysis. But Freud discovered very early in his work that resistance, especially transference resistance, impairs the patient's capacity to assimilate and integrate truths imparted by means of interpretation. In his comments on the Dora case (1905a) Freud noted that she had terminated treatment because he had paid insufficient attention to resistance. He also said that he had not succeeded in mastering the transference, a technical "failure" which led Dora to act out her recollections and fantasies instead of reproducing them verbally in the treatment.

Thus, in those early days of psychoanalytic discovery, Freud learned that the epigram "The truth shall set you free" had its limitations. He said:

> If knowledge about the unconscious were as important for the patient as people inexperienced in psychoanalysis imagine, listening to lectures or reading books would be enough to cure him. Such measures, however, have as much influence on the symptoms of nervous illness as a distribution of menu-cards in a time of famine has upon hunger. (1910:225)

When Freud learned how to master the transference resistance he understood that the ego had to be readied to accept the interpretation.

He inserted analysis of resistance before interpretation of content. The consideration of readying the ego also led him to evolve his ideas about tact and timing and the importance of working through. Technique, then, was designed to conquer the resistances, the impediments to interpretation. Thereafter an interpretation, to be correct, had to be correct not only in content but in timing as well. To that, Freud added *working through,* a process of uncovering the same constellation of id wishes from many angles until all impediments to rational examination of them are overcome.

Yet Freud found instances in his clinical experience when working through did not take place. In his treatment of the Wolf Man, Freud was forced to take desperate measures—to promise a cure for a psychosomatic ailment and to set a deadline for termination. How much this succeeded in forcing the patient to work through his resistances remains a serious question. It is now believed that the Wolf Man's capacities to absorb interpretations and to work them through were less than Freud thought.

Nevertheless, Freud's concern with techniques that would pave the way for interpretation led to refinements in technique that made interpretation more effective in many instances. Interpretation remained the prime tool. All that changed in psychoanalytic technique was *when* interpretation was to be made. It remained a basic tenet that all distortions could be corrected by exposure to the "light of day," that is, to the rational, conscious ego. Thus childhood misperception and fantasy would be corrected by the more experienced adult ego.

Much of the methodology of psychoanalysis is based upon assumptions having to do with these distortions in the mental life of the neurotic patient. These assumptions are:

1. that distortions in perception—mistaking present for past—create transference phenomena;
2. that all patients, understandably, defend against anxiety and thereby present resistances in the analytic situation;
3. that, in time, neurosis, transference, and resistance begin to coincide in the analytic process to become transference neurosis and transference resistance; and
4. that unconscious fantasy plays a determining role in mental life.

Since Freud worked out his theory of technique in the period from approximately 1910 to 1913, he did not yet have the theoretical tools to enable him to put them in the frame of reference of a superordinate structure. Even when he did allude to the *gesamt Ich* in 1921, he did so in passing because he was no longer intent upon elaborating technique. In essence, Freud's technical innovations taught us that truths must await psychological readiness to absorb them. In fact he did articulate that those patients who had to be dismissed as unanalyzable were not possessed of the same capacities as those who could be analyzed. He framed his ideas about the differences between these two categories of patients in object relations terms—those who could and those who could not form a transference. This speaks to competent development in the one instance, and to malformed development in the other.

Here we merely extend those technical and diagnostic considerations. The underlying philosophy that technique has to be tailored to the capacity of the patient to use interpretation remains the same. Now that we include the understructured patient we find that there is a wider range in that capacity—from the ability to use interpretation, as the neurotic patient does, to having to acquire such ability in the course of the therapy, to an inability that calls for different technical measures. Transposed into our terms, Freud's technical precepts depend upon the competence of the patient's superordinate ego to deal with malformations in development.

This strongly suggests that, in order to proceed correctly, it is now essential to take into account not only defense and transference resistance, but developmental vicissitudes and the capacity of the superordinate ego to organize them. What is required of the therapist is a thorough grasp of developmental theory in order to be alert to the vicissitudes of development in a given individual. And even beyond that, keen attunement to the patient's capacities is a skill that must be assiduously developed in the therapist.

The capacity of the superordinate ego to organize developmental malformations determines the limits of the patient's comprehension, grasp of the issues, and ability to process the information. That is another way of saying that developmental issues determine the patient's availability for interpretation. This does not exclude transference neurosis and transference resistance in the structured patient, for those considerations are adequately subsumed as developmental issues.

These thoughts are consonant with what we know about growth in general. One cannot burden the child at the level of the first organizer with the fact that the face he or she is smiling at is that of a stranger. Neither will the child at the level of the second organizer respond to assurances of friendly intent on the part of the stranger. The oedipal child is not instantly and permanently reassured by the friendliness of the parent of the same sex. It takes a long time for the adolescent to be convinced that the good enough parents are not really impeding autonomy even though his or her anxiety about it causes the child-becoming-an-adult to project restraining wishes upon the parents.

In the less than neurotic structures many behaviors which look like conflict, defense, and resistance may reflect, instead, organizational incapacity to deal with developmental malformation and, in the present, to absorb and process information. The existence of a high level of intelligence may mislead the therapist into believing that comprehension and integration by an adequately functioning superordinate ego is taking place. Where, however, a capacity does not yet exist—analogous to the inability of the three-month-old to acquire the libidinal object proper—we are not dealing with an intractable resistance, but with a developmental malformation which will not respond to interpretive efforts.

Probably the most reliable indicator of whether the level of organization renders the individual capable of integrating the "facts" presented is the level of object relations within the totality of ego organization. At the level of self and object constancy, which we assume obtains in the structured patient, there is a tacit assumption on the part of the patient that another person has needs. Such patients may accept the necessities of the fee, the fixed appointments, and other arrangements that surround the treatment process with bad grace, but they understand them. The understructured patient, as we have said before (1979), is asked to function beyond his or her capacity in those matters.

For example, both types of patient may dread that the analyst's needs will enter the picture. Often, with the structured patient, this fear becomes prominent when the patient is getting better and is beginning to feel gratitude. The better-structured patient is likely, then, to bring up material derived from anal conflicts because a genuine wish to give is coming to the fore, in conflict with the fear that one's generosity will impel one to give away too much. Understructured patients are more likely to fear demands as repetitions of experiences in the real world where more had been demanded of them than their phase-appropriate capacities were able to tolerate. Giving, to them, is concrete; it means loss of body parts and sometimes of one's very self.

Analysts have long admired Ella Freeman Sharpe's skill in attunement, exemplified in the well-known response to the patient who covered his eyes with a red handkerchief (1950:58). She asked, "And is the headache helped that way?" There are patients who could have responded positively to the more challenging "Why?" Sharpe's more gentle intervention provided greater therapeutic opportunity. It was less likely to evoke a defensive response in the structured patient, and, although Sharpe did not know it conceptually, it left room for a patient with a lower level of object relations to respond differently. With our current knowledge, one might suspect that a man who is so involved with his wife's menstrual cycle is not separated from her. In Sharpe's time this was regarded as an identification, implying a greater degree of separation and individuation than we might today find to exist.

One may wonder what enabled Sharpe to know that the patient could not respond to challenge and confrontation at that point. While we have no answer from her directly, we know from her writings that she was always closely attuned to her patients; indeed, she coined phrases such as "Go with the patient" and "Do not pounce" to illuminate this precept. In our more sophisticated terms, she did not demand more of the patient than the patient's capacities could provide. He was not obliged to gratify the analyst's therapeutic zeal.

In apparently well-functioning patients malformations are not always prominent. A patient whose children had reached school age announced happily, "My wife is going back to work and my income will double." In his great relief from the strain of being the family's sole provider, he thus reveals that he is profoundly merged with his wife. He is unaware of the import of what he has said and certainly does not raise it as an issue that troubles him—quite the contrary, it pleases him. Therefore it is untimely and inappropriate to inform him that he has made a slip of the tongue that reveals that his self and object images are merged. The therapist, noting this, opens pathways in the hope that, ultimately, the problem will enter the transference. An appropriate beginning, for example, would be "I had not realized how worried you have been about finances." This statement focuses on where the patient feels the anxiety. It follows Sharpe's counsel not to pounce. The therapist who pounces on a slip of the tongue may trap the patient into facing a truth for which the ego is not yet prepared. This may be compared with the patient who hears his or her own slips and calls them to the analyst's attention in a true working alliance.

In this case the separation-individuation problem will emerge in transferential form as the patient experiences that the therapist understands his anxiety. It may appear, to cite one possibility, when payment for a missed session becomes an issue. In 1979 we described the not uncommon thought disorder that comes to light around the fee during a patient's vacation. The patient said, "You don't pay me when you go away, so why should I pay you when I go away?"

Another patient blithely informed the therapist that she had voluntarily made a change in her work schedule which would necessitate changing one of her therapy sessions. She had not discussed this with the therapist. She behaved as though she expected him to comply with her change and found it impossible to believe that he could not make that change in his own schedule. In her mind the therapist was able to do whatever she wished.

That patient's problem *is* in the transference, it is true, but it cannot be met by interpretation. She is living in the immediacy of experience, not in the structure, and so she needs a response which addresses the experience she has at the moment—frustration, anger, and disappointment. To say, "You made this change without discussing it with me first," is, of course, accurate, but it scolds the patient for not behaving on a higher level of object relations than she possesses.

Now we even question whether uncovering childhood memories as distinct events is viable even in the psychoanalysis of the structured patient. As Kris (1956c) points out, to pursue repressed memory is a simplistic and unworkable version of the analytic process. He showed that rarely is a single childhood memory reliable and waiting in the unconscious to be uncovered as it actually occurred. There are *patterns* of childhood experience that alter with time and with the developing child's increasing capacity to process experience. Thus childhood experience is reworked many times, becoming condensed with later experience as the organizing process incorporates later events with the earlier ones. Experience is thereby not only processed when it takes place, it is reprocessed as development proceeds.

Our addition to Kris' important observation is that the organizing process begins from below—that is, that the patterning is already determined, in a certain sense, before the experience takes place. This is attributable to three factors:

1. The innate endowment, including the capacity to extract from the environment, directs the child to interact with the object world.
2. Coenesthetic sensing exerts a silent influence upon the style of processing experience.
3. The patterning of object relations, begun to be fashioned in early infancy, continues to be shaped when the diacritic mode is superimposed upon the coenesthetic.

Consideration of these factors modifies the concept of psychoanalysis as a process of "excavation." The search for the truth as the key to freedom from the neurosogenic influence of repressed material becomes an undertaking of a different sort. We search less for memories, more for patterning; for relatively fixed programs; for clues through transferential behavior about the nature of the "slot" into which the analyst is cast. The level of function achieved by the superordinate ego determines whether the therapist encounters strongly fixed, ineradicable assumptions about objects or whether alteration of patterning is possible.

The concept of a superordinate ego secures Kris' position. It relegates "the truth" to secondary importance. What is primary is how the truth is perceived and in what frame of reference it is registered. The therapeutic task is to facilitate the functioning of the superordinate ego so that experience is processed more realistically. In other words, therapy is a process whereby the patient's capacity to bring past and present experiences into a more harmonious form of organization is quickened.

Throughout, we have attempted to convey that the therapist must acquire a sense of developmental levels, capacities, organizational functions, in order to be able to recognize which are within reach and which are still out of sight. The therapeutic process, at its best, is one in which growth proceeds at a pace determined by the patient's superordinate ego. This is vastly different from a therapy based upon revealed truth. It happens that, with structured patients, properly timed interpretation *is* the technique that promotes growth; the infantile wishes, fantasies, and transference distortions are comfortably laid to rest by the adult ego. But with understructured patients interpretation is not usually effective. If we interpret without regard for the difference in capacity to process, we give the patient that which Kris (1956c) described as an id vernacular, at best. At worst, we confuse the patient and precipitate decompensation.

CHAPTER 15
TRACKING

WE HAVE suggested the term *tracking* for the therapeutic process involving mutual cuing. It is an interactive dialogue conducted on many levels, particularly useful for the understructured patient who needs to be understood with exquisite attunement.

Freud discovered, through his clinical experience, that not every patient could be treated by the analytic method. It could only be effective for the patient with an "unmodified" ego. In the two-week trial analysis that he used for diagnostic purposes, he endeavored to distinguish between those who could endure the rigors of the analytic method and those whose egos were not equal to the task. We now refer to the former as well structured and to the latter as understructured.

The tracking process is applicable in the treatment of the analyzable, structured patient as well as the understructured, but it takes a somewhat different form in each. In treating the structured patient, we take it for granted that the spoken word is the clearest form of communication. Yet nonverbal forms of communication take place in every treatment situation. Affect, especially, is more often communicated through transference (and countertransference) and through body movement and gesture than through words. But the understructured patient whose foothold in the secondary process is less secure and who has barely, if at all, reached the level of Spitz's third organizer tends to use verbal communication reluctantly. Without much conviction, and therefore lacking both content and affect which the therapist needs in order to understand completely, such patients use the spoken word in compliance with the wishes of the listener.

One of Freud's major technical devices—free association—is based on the fact that associations are not really free because the analyzable patient can loosen cathexis to the secondary process but never loses that cathexis completely. There are always connections which the "working" patient or the analyst will discern sooner or later. Kris (1956a) thought that connection is so important that he modified the purpose of the basic rule by stressing the priority of reestablishing broken connections over recovering that which had been repressed. With analyzable patients, these connections already possess considerable coherence and, in addition, the analyst can rely upon such patients' egos to organize data. These are capacities which are fixed and stable in the structured patients, but which the understructured patients possess in varying degrees, ranging from almost none at all to that which approaches the competence of the more structured patient. Therefore, especially in the treatment of the understructured patient, correct tracking requires that the therapist be able to distinguish among defense (resistance), impulse, need for affirmation, need for empathy, and need for growth-promoting frustration. Only with these distinctions can the process be uniquely tailored to the individual needs of the patient.

We shall describe in detail the differences in tracking in psychoanalysis proper and in the psychotherapy of the understructured patient.

Despite the precaution of a two-week trial analysis, Freud often erred in his diagnosis, as do analysts to this very day. Of Freud's five reported cases, two of them—Schreber and Little Hans—were not treated by him directly. Schreber was an acknowledged psychotic whose "analysis" Freud conducted through Schreber's memoirs; Little Hans was a child whose father analyzed him under Freud's "supervision." Of the patients Freud did treat—Dora, the Rat Man, and the Wolf Man—probably none would meet today's criteria for analyzability.

The case of the Rat Man provides the clearest illustration of the problems inherent in the technique of tracking. Freud relied upon the capacity of an unmodified ego to provide the connecting threads which could produce some semblance of order and coherence in otherwise chaotic material. But it is now believed that Freud may have been mistaken in his diagnosis, that the Rat Man was not capable of organizing his own chaotic processes. Thus, Freud's pursuit of the Rat Man's impossibly elaborate ideas about repaying his debt led him on a wild goose chase. Freud said:

> It would not surprise me to hear that at this point the reader had ceased to

be able to follow. For even the detailed account which the patient gave me of the external events of these days and of his reactions to them was full of self-contradictions and sounded hopelessly confused. It was only when he told me the story for the third time that I could get him to realize its obscurities and could lay bare the errors of memory and the displacements in which he had become involved. I shall spare myself the trouble of reproducing these details . . . and I will only add that at the end of this second session the patient behaved as though he were dazed and bewildered. He repeatedly addressed me as "Captain," probably because at the beginning of the hour I had told him that I myself was not fond of cruelty like Captain N., and that I had no intention of tormenting him unnecessarily. (1909:169)

Freud made a connection between the facts that the patient called him Captain and that he, Freud, had mentioned Captain N. during the session. This might be called tracking on the narrow level. But on the broad level Freud pressed the Rat Man for a coherent story, overlooking the fact that this precipitated an ego regression which resulted in the condensation. If he had possessed today's knowledge, this would have alerted him to the fact that fragmentation had begun. Ultimately, it was Freud who made the connection, since the Rat Man proved to be incapable of ordering the material.

The following is a portion of a case which illustrates how a patient with a better foothold in the secondary process does order her material in the midst of the "chaos" of free association:

A woman who had been in long-term treatment reported a dream: "My mother was seriously ill and in bed. I crawled into bed with her, cradled her in my arms, tried to get her to look at me and to speak. She did not, but each time that I thought she was gone, she would make some movement, indicating that she was still alive; but I could not get her to respond to me." The patient then voiced the fears that she experienced upon awakening—that the dream might indicate a globally passive wish to be taken care of, and that it also might indicate homosexual wishes. Then she added, "I can't think of anything else that you would want me to tell you."

Since the patient had a long history of conflict between compliance and rebellion, which was frequently reproduced in the transference, the analyst responded with, "Let's see where your own thoughts take you, apart from what you may think I want." By this time in the treatment the patient had become a truly "working" patient. She responded positively, stopped musing on the dream, and went on with her concerns of the moment. She described some difficulties with her children, another problem about a presentation she had to make to the president of the company she works for, a brief marital spat, some negative reaction to something the analyst had said a week earlier.

As she continued with these associations, she interrupted herself at one point to say, "It's funny, but suddenly I know what that dream is about. I am really quite anxious about tomorrow's presentation to the president of the company. I wish I did not have to make it, and I have been trying to figure some way out of the entire deal, despite the fact that the presentation was my own idea and probably will help me in my work to a considerable extent. So I am crawling into my mother's bed, trying to avoid the task which worries me so, and looking to my mother to affirm my ducking out, which she always did when she was alive."

Her anxiety diminished when she made this interpretation. She commented that she felt better. The analyst had only to add that she had once again reproduced her conflict between compliance and rebellion, between wish for connection with her mother, who had been unattuned to her need to function autonomously, and her own need to function. The conflict resulted in anxiety, defended against by the regressive wishes which her mother had always fostered. The analyst is represented in the dream as her mother. This is a condensation that depicts the conflict—the mother as she was and the analyst who is represented as neutral between her wish to function and her wish to regress to a helpless state. (Obviously, there are many other aspects of this dream which will need to be dealt with, but only when the patient's ego is ready to consider the additional problems, free of the compliance-rebellion conflict so prominent in her life and so much in evidence here.)

What is it that enabled this patient to find a way of ordering the chaotic material in one (important) area, to find a focus which led her to an interpretation that relieved the anxiety? She found a connecting thread to her immediate present and to the past, one which made good sense to her. We contrast this with the Rat Man, whose intention to repay the trivial loan led him astray in ever-widening spirals. It is precisely these kinds of clinical observations that led us to postulate a superordinate ego, one which can arrange adaptive order, as in this instance, and can even create a more useful form of maladaptive order by means of defenses. Because the Rat Man could not do either, he rambled on endlessly, becoming more and more confused to the point of utter incoherence. In the structured patient, by contrast, the tracking process has an ally in the superordinate structure which is engaged continuously in the process of organization. This enables the person to discern connections or at least "leak" them to the analyst by means of free associations. Such a patient can also create defenses where necessary so that fragmentation is not a danger.

Psychotherapy with the understructured patient, therefore, must be different because the patient is a less competent partner in the therapeutic alliance. This decreased level of competence requires that the therapist be capable of attunement to the failures in organization and of finding ways to promote growth.

Isolating the component factors, we may speak of coherent organization in the structured patient, the consequence of an adequate superordinate ego which can perform the following tasks:

1. Provide a counterforce to an inner urge.
2. Free associate. Implicit here is the existence of a capacity to reveal coherent connective threads, even in the state of loosened cathexis of secondary process thought.
3. Possess the capacity to become increasingly aware of both the urges and the existence of a counterforce.
4. Develop a capacity for positive object cathexis in the transference sufficient to enable the patient to tolerate both anxiety and frustration in favor of larger, long-term goals.

Patients with such capacities can work more usefully with interpretive techniques. Juxtaposing this with Freud's observation that the fixation points in the narcissistic neuroses arise much earlier than in the transference neuroses, it is logical to suggest that a vastly lesser capacity to organize mental processes exists because of those fixations in early development. The effects of this in the understructured patient posit the following:

1. There may be no counterforce to an inner urge. Such structures

would include impulse disorders and those aberrant processes which may have become ego syntonic.

2. Since the capacity to organize mental processes coherently is deficient or malformed, free association will reflect chaotic disorganization, with the result that no useful connecting threads can be discerned.

3. The capacity to make connections, that is, true insight as differentiated from what Kris (1956c) called an empty id vernacular, has not been achieved. True semantic communication, reflecting full affective cathexis of a high level of object relations, has also not been achieved.

4. With malformations in structure having had their inception early in development, the existence of a positive balance over negative affects toward self and object cannot be assumed.

While we have attempted here to elucidate that there is a fundamental difference between techniques for treating understructured patients and techniques which are more productive with structured patients, the reality of clinical practice reveals that most of the time there are combinations of defensive patterns intermingled with developmental malformations, and that treatment techniques must therefore fluctuate between dealing with each in turn.

Such conceptual differences about structure necessitate changes in technique, precisely as Freud urged (1917b:422–423). The underlying motif is drawn not only from increased knowledge about development per se, but also from reaching into the composition of the ego itself and its component parts. Probably, at this state of our knowledge, we are only scratching the surface. But we are equipped to consider a number of factors. Has the object world been discerned—that is, are object representations established? Does development include cathexis of a single primary object—that is, have object relations been established? Is there evenly distributed positive cathexis of both the self representations and the object representations? How clear do the ego boundaries appear? How well have the various differentiation processes been accomplished? Is there a reasonable capacity to delay and postpone drive discharge? What is the affective range—only from good to bad, or is there a more complete affective repertory? What is the regressive potential—is there a regressive floor, or does it dissolve into primary process?

We have already said that the therapist must be able to tolerate uncertainty. It is this tolerance that enables him or her to track the patient's responses, to regard them as reflective of a given developmental level, to grope for understanding, and to respond in a fashion attuned both to the needs of that level and to the task of promoting growth to the next level. In such a process, those individuals who possess a more integrated organizing capacity—that is, a better-functioning super-ordinate ego—can be expected to assimilate truths in ways which differ from those whose organizing capacity labors under handicaps of poorly completed developmental tasks. It is the therapist's task to seek out and provide the best mix of benign climate and appropriate therapeutic nudge forward. To accomplish this the therapist must provide precisely titrated frustration, enough to stimulate growth and promote inter-nalizing processes which will bring external, regulating disciplinary measures under the internal control of the individual, but not more than the patient's capacity can utilize successfully.

It is perhaps in relation to this last point that the many jokes about the stony-faced analyst tell us an important truth. Psychoanalytic tech-niques, such as abstinence and accompanying frustration, that are ap-plicable and necessary in the treatment of the more highly organized structures, provide more than the optimal amount of frustration in other instances. Where inappropriately applied, abstinence replicates negative primary object experiences; therefore, it is not growth pro-moting.

We refer again to a case described in chapter 12. Here the focus is limited to one aspect of this patient's developmental malformations, one that reflects the probability that there was an inadequate practicing subphase. The practicing subphase is the period in which there is a great leap forward in the quickening and functioning of autonomous ego apparatuses. A successful practicing subphase provides positive experiences that will endure in the self representation. Close proximity to the primary object is essential to success, while impairment is the consequence of seriously unattuned partnering. The mother must be able to engage and disengage in a fluctuating rhythm which coordinates with the child's capabilities and mood of the moment. Even as she lets go, the mother must be ever present lest the toddler take himself too far for his psychic capacity to tolerate. In these distancing trials, the child takes the initiative, an active role that leads to the elated investment in the exercise of autonomous functioning, heralding the "escape" from symbiosis. This leads to a peak of healthy narcissistic self-valuation when all goes well.

It is to be borne in mind, in considering the problems of any adult patient, that they derive from the total organization of experience, not from one isolated subphase of the separation-individuation process. The danger of attempting to correlate early development with adult behavior in a one-to-one fashion cannot be overstressed. Even where we know of inadequacies in a given phase or subphase, we know also that development has proceeded. The consequences of inadequate experiences become incorporated in the ongoing process of organization, which also includes adaptation and corrective experience. Mahler believes that an adequate rapprochement subphase can correct some of the inadequacies of the earlier subphases. Our difference with her reduces to a matter of degree. We have already indicated our belief that traits accrue in the self-images that do not become eradicated by later experience, although they most certainly can become modified if the structure capable of producing modifications exists. Nevertheless, the point we wish to stress here is that it is an absurd oversimplification to believe that one can treat each phase and subphase in an orderly fashion as though an adult patient can relive early experience in a better way.

The key technical problem in the case to be presented is that there is unlimited regressive potential—a low regressive floor. Under the stress of anxiety the patient regresses to a "wooden" state as a defense against an unconsciously wished-for merger. Despite that, there is a restitutive capacity which has enabled this man to grow, to develop, to proceed through the subphases. Perhaps it would be more accurate to say that he limped through the subphases.

This patient rarely feels elated. There is a noticeable upsurge of positive feelings when he receives affirmation from the therapist or from his supervisor, but this is far from self-sustaining. This indicates that self-esteem is not internalized and metabolized as part of his own structure, but requires continuous reinforcement from external sources. In the brief dialogue to follow, there is a suggestion of practicing subphase inadequacy. The thrust of the therapist's effort is to encourage reorganization in the area impaired by subphase failure, with full recognition that problems arose in other aspects of development as well. Although the patient's negative, depressed self-image could well have originated in the practicing subphase, each reflection of other subphase inadequacies must be dealt with as it arises in the treatment process. Rarely do they arise in an orderly progression.

The patient is a man competent in his profession, with a history of frequent job loss. At times he becomes, as he describes it, "wooden." At those times he spends days in his apartment alone except occasionally to go out for food. The symptom is understood as a defense against further regression because anxiety is at the level of annihilation, not signal anxiety. The therapeutic purpose is to promote anxiety tolerance while helping him continue to function where possible. Some dialogue follows:

PATIENT: I've got an important report coming due and I will have to bury myself in work this weekend.

THERAPIST: Oh, what's it about?

PATIENT: It's a report that the vice president will need for the next meeting.

THERAPIST: Is this unusual, or is it an ongoing matter?

PATIENT: Oh, it's the annual report due this time every year. As a matter of fact I've been collecting the data I need for several weeks now.

THERAPIST: But you will still have to bury yourself?

The therapist does not want to challenge the functioning capacity and so refrains from asking *why* he has to bury himself even though he already has the data for the report. This leaves room both for reconsideration of the "burial process" if that should become possible, or acceptance of it if this is the only way the patient can continue to function.

PATIENT: As a matter of fact, I was just asking myself why I put it in such extremes. I can easily see my friends on Saturday afternoon as usual.

THERAPIST: Well, you do tend to approach tasks as though they all require maximum effort from you. Perhaps one day you may begin to feel

that you can get this done without having to give up all of your
other activity.

PATIENT: I've begun to wonder about that myself.

THERAPIST: It's a good thing to wonder about.

No interpretation is attempted, no conclusion is sought. What is
being worked on here is the pathological direction that development
has taken. More than simply drive, conflict, defense, and resistance
have to be considered. Especially important are self and object relations.
The self representations are insufficiently cathected with positive value;
the object representations are overly cathected, and with negative value.
Therefore, other persons are experienced as demanding, hostile, and
overwhelming. The therapeutic thrust in this interchange is for the
therapist to avoid "playing the game" as Fenichel (1941) put it. Specifically, the therapist must avoid replication of negative experience with
the demanding primary object lest he also become all-powerful and
negatively cathected.

This is an example of the way in which appropriate tracking can
preserve the benign climate even while demands are being made of the
patient. The patient is asked to consider whether the burial is necessary,
but in a way which leaves open the possibility that he may find that
it is essential in order to preserve his functioning level, which is of
primary importance. Once it is established that he need not bury
himself, that issue is left open for the patient to address in the future.
Since there is no doubt about his capacity to perfom his duties well,
the hope here is that such discussion will point up his dread of taking
action in the presence of the object, in this case his supervisor. In the
therapeutic interchange, therefore, any initiative he displays is carefully
nourished.

This is not to say that the symbolism in the patient's statement
about burial is disregarded. Its importance promises to be enormous,
but it is too early to burden the patient with this matter at his present
level of organization. The hypothesis is that it represents identification
with a deceased parent. This is exactly the kind of truth that would
overburden his fragile organization. He would not be overwhelmed by
such disclosure but would probably be happy to discuss it at great
length with all his superb capacity for defensive intellectualization.

More often than is perhaps realized, truths are excavated in ways that cannot be therapeutically effective; they are uncovered but cannot be worked through.

If this patient has an operative superordinate ego, then repeated experiences of successful completion of tasks might promote the internalization of positive self-experience. At this stage, he requires far more external confirmation than a person who has more successfully negotiated the Fulcrum. We do not provide praise from without, although the problem in early development arose because exactly that was lacking at the phase-appropriate time. It cannot help to provide it belatedly. He must acquire it by his own self-evaluation. As the treatment process proceeds, he will be asked again later whether he still finds it necessary to exert maximum effort to perform routine tasks. If this therapeutic thrust succeeds, he may find that it is not.

Another patient constantly seeks for the interpretation which will make her feel better, that is, the magic word that will cure her of her depression. But it is always the therapist, or another external person, upon whom this task devolves. Internal mastery of affect, or even the process of struggling with affect, is not a function which she can perceive as her own. The therapist asks, "How can I help you feel better?" The response is, "I want you to *make* me feel better." The therapist asks, "Do you think you might want to help the process along?" Thus the therapist avoids disclaiming the responsibility, although obviously not accepting it either, and tries to maintain the essential therapeutic alliance by avoiding outright rejection of the patient's wish. There is considerable difference in asking the patient whether she might *want* to help the process along and whether she might *try* to help. The latter demands more.

What is involved here is the developmental sequence which optimally produces mastery of affect. Mastery is vastly different from the frightened compliance of the previous patient. This patient has a better capacity to extract from the environment; but her focus is on purely alloplastic adaptation. Provisions must come from the external world because she lacks the ability to grasp that adaptation also involves autoplastic processes.

Another patient began treatment at age sixteen, while a sophomore in high school. Regarded as the dolt in a successful business family, he was brought to treatment because he was failing in school. He was a sturdy, stocky youngster who tried hard at whatever he did. Some connection with the therapist was established by means of his discussion of his attempt to make the football team. Although the therapist had never played football, he was able to engage the patient in a discussion of the best way to tackle the ball carrier. The patient invariably grabbed the other boy around the shoulders, an inefficient way of tackling that terrified his coach, who feared that the patient would be injured.

Because of the nature of the fixed unconscious assumptions in this patient's structure, the external object was invariably experienced as intruding upon the self representation. Where identification with the aggressor is established in normal growth, the object representation is admitted into the structure with positive cathexis, ultimately resulting in the capacity to transfer a function of the object representation to the self representation. Where this has not occurred, for whatever reason, identity formation goes forward more as a bootstrap operation, with minimal object cathexis or with negative object cathexis. In such circumstances, object representations are perceived as hampering identity formation. Then the growth-promoting process of mutually enhancing positive cathexis of self representations and object representations is blocked, and the balance of this essential line of development is skewed. Incidentally, football is a game which might have been designed as a metaphor for such psychological skewing, since the major objective is to get to the goal by getting the hampering object out of the way.

While the therapist was able to establish himself as helpful in a nonintrusive fashion for this patient, of itself, such experience is not a technique which can promote the internalization of a "better" experience. Therefore it could not be expected to extend to other situations. "Reparative" experiences such as this do not correct assumptions which have become fixed. The therapist must continue to work with the fact that object representations constitute a threat to identity formation despite the fact that objects are needed. The therapeutic alliance is burdened with the task of continuously proving the absence of threat in the therapeutic situation.

The therapist circumvented the threat in this instance by his willingness to continue discussing how the patient could remain on the team. Parenthetically, the therapist also worried about the possibility of brain concussion, but was driven to support the patient's "practicing" needs—that is, his ambitious strivings—and to hope for the best. This attempt to help him master a difficult and worrisome situation came to appear to the patient as the opposite of the coach's and family's representation of him as a dolt. It reinforced the therapeutic alliance and permitted treatment to continue.

Developmental object relations theory in general, and the concept of a superordinate ego in particular, provide opportunity for more effective work in dealing with conflict and resistance, since they are perceived as part of a whole structure, with the therapeutic address focused upon the whole person rather than upon separate psychic institutions.

Freud's discovery that his hysterical patients might not have suffered an actual incestuous advance forced him to relocate the field of conflict. Instead of seeing the ego in conflict with external reality—the incestuous object—the fact that the "event" occurred in fantasy as a result of a wish made it necessary to locate the conflict between two of the systems, that is, between ego and id or ego and superego.

Intersystemic conflict became central to psychoanalytic thought. In working with intersystemic conflict, the analyst works with the "rational ego," aiding it to confront either id wishes or the punishing superego. "Where id was there shall ego be" (1933:80) reflected the triumph of conscious rational thinking and behavior; this was fostered by the benign, accepting attitude of the analyst toward hitherto frowned-upon sexuality.

In that philosophy of treatment, the analyst and the reality-based ego formed an alliance. Thus we come to understand how it was that gifted theorists of technique such as Fenichel, Greenson, and Menninger, could think of the defensive ego as the enemy, of resistance as oppositional and destructive. When conflict is located between two of the systems, then the rescuer must become allied with the one "good" system, the rational ego, against the "bad" other system, id or superego.

Hartmann found a theoretical explanation for the clinical fact that many patients' behaviors failed to follow the simple yet attractive formula of aiding the ego in its struggles. The ego, thought to be ally and partner in the therapeutic process, could itself be in serious disarray because of developmental malformations. It could even be in conflict within itself.

It is noteworthy that in 1921, before he presented the structural theory, Freud was already integrating his ideas about structure without yet being able to identify its components. He even suggested that there could be intrasystemic conflict, a matter that Hartmann was to develop many years later. But the conflict that Freud referred to in 1921 was between the ego and the ego ideal. Two years later he was to equate ego ideal and superego, thus changing the locale of that particular conflict from intrasystemic to intersystemic. It remained for Hartmann to rediscover intrasystemic conflict. But by then, because so much more was known about the ego, that kind of conflict was seen somewhat differently. Now we know that there can be conflict between ego functions and between the representations that are internalized there.

That there can be intrasystemic conflict alters the simple theoretical idea that, technically, the analyst can always rely upon the rational ego as an ally. By this discovery, or rediscovery, an era came to an end. Now we have to decide, diagnostically, when there is structure that can be counted on and when the ego itself is so involved in conflict that it needs therapeutic help, hopefully to become that strong, rational ego that analysts took for granted several decades ago. Now we see that even the adaptive function can be compromised, impeded, or distorted, resulting in malformed organization. In this sense we may say that the Rat Man's reference to Freud as Captain reflects a distorted attempt at adaptation. Thus, we cannot rely upon ego processes to be wholly consonant with reality. We must think of the ego's relation to reality as a "vision of reality," as Schafer does.

Clearly, this introduces complexities in the techniques for addressing conflict. To rely upon interpretation of the transference neurosis to demonstrate to the patient that the analyst is not the primary object is a beguilingly attractive oversimplification of the patient's difficulties and of the therapeutic task. That there can be ego elements aligned against other ego elements, as well as against the other psychic institutions, provides a new perspective. For example, opposition, heretofore believed to represent resistance, has now to be thought about more selectively. The stubborn "No" can reflect the fact that growth is in progress. This dictates the paradoxical technique of aiding "resistance" as part of the therapeutic process in instances where it reflects not defense, but developmental gain.

Conflict impinges upon the capacity for orderly, coherent arrangement, imposing its effects directly upon that process. The superordinate ego either fails, succeeds, or makes some arrangement between those two extremes. Conflict then results in impeded function of the whole person and needs to be seen in that context. We know from Spitz that organization has already taken place before the appearance of the smiling response. This permits us safely to assume that the organizing process is in effect from the beginning of life.

In the process of development, differentiation and integration occur simultaneously. Thereby, in the very process of differentiation, the seeds of the next level of integration already exist. This provides the therapist with the opportunity to consider all the interlocking elements of organization simultaneously, including fundamental programming, organization of drives, developing autonomy and identity formation, external influence, innate endowment, and the current level of the organizing process as it functions in resistance and transference manifestations.

As an example, therapists often attempt to interpret reality to patients, or even try to represent reality—that is, they attempt to appeal to the rational ego. The function of the therapist is, rather, to try to provide a bridge to reality in a process attuned to the patient's capacity to cross that bridge. Often enough the patient may not be able to do so, in which case the malformation in organization must be addressed, or, to state it another way, the failure of the superordinate ego to comprehend must become the focus.

The football aspirant mentioned earlier wanted to buy a very expensive and exotic motor car, many years later. In one session he decried his own wish; the car was much too expensive, required too much care, he did not need that kind of trouble. Yet in the very next session, when the therapist simply recalled the patient's own words of the day before, the patient became upset at the notion that the therapist did not want him to have so nice a car. The tracking error might be excused on the premise that this patient had had long experience with the therapist as a nonintrusive object, but it remains a tracking error.

Instead of repeating the patient's statement of the day before, a therapist attuned to the patient's uneasy capacity to attain and maintain coherence could have said, "It's hard to come to a conclusion about this, isn't it?" When, subsequently, that was said, the patient responded with, "No it's very easy to come to a conclusion. I come to ten different conclusions about it, and it only takes me ten minutes to do so." Here the patient begins a rational confrontation from within, holding out hope that there will be an alteration in the direction of rationality without the therapist's intrusion upon processes that proceed more successfully within the ego.

There are situations in which the therapist must stand for reality, but these are few. Failure to pay the fee is one example; an attack upon the therapist's person or possessions is another; and, of course, suicidal intentions must be thwarted if possible. In all such instances, however, the therapist loses an integral aspect of his professional stance, that of trying to remain attuned to the patient's position in the specific situation. The patient's difficulty in paying the fee, for example, is best dealt with by understanding why it is difficult for him and by helping the patient with it. This is paradoxical because it cannot be done without insisting upon payment. To defer payment would infantilize the patient in the very process of attempting to promote growth.

> A patient described an argument with her husband, out of which she wondered whether her preoccupation with the therapist might not have led her to distance herself from her husband. The therapist used the opportunity to draw in some dream material and to connect this with the facts of the patient's history, thereby confirming the likelihood of the patient's observation. The patient distorted this to mean that the therapist did not want her to be interested in him. She accused him angrily of theorizing and intellectualizing instead of having flesh and blood feelings.

Although the intervention subsequently proved to be correct, it was a tracking error to have introduced material which the patient had "forgotten" at that moment. Also to be noted is that patients often do tell us truths about ourselves. Sometimes we do intellectualize when the affective climate becomes too warm.

But it may be too strong a judgment to label this an error. Out of such trials we learn how best to address a patient's specific problems. These probes produce reactions which can usually be absorbed if the benign climate and the therapeutic alliance have been sedulously guarded. Flexible attunement to the patient's responses is crucially important, as this is precisely how one learns to work *with* the patient's resistances and not against them.

But what do we mean by flexible attunement? And do we really need yet another term in addition to the popular ones—*intuition* and *empathy*? We believe that we do. The basis for our modification of classical technique for the understructured patient lies in knowledge of developmental processes, their phases and subphases. We use that knowledge as a foundation that is considerably more reliable than some mysterious intuitive talent. Intuition runs the unacceptable risk of coun-tertransference behavior that may be damaging. "I tried it and it worked" is too primitive given our present state of knowledge.

Empathy, which refers to the capacity to "feel in" with another person, is closely related to intuition. It involves identifications, which can also lead to countertransference behavior which may be damaging. Some theorists, Loewald in particular, have even suggested that the therapist must be capable of merging boundaries. It seems to us that this would only be desirable in the treatment of psychosis where there is need for a symbiotic experience out of which the patient will, hope-fully, emerge. It goes without saying that if the therapist is to merge, he or she must be certain that such regression is in the service of the ego and can be reversed at will. For outpatient borderline pathology, the therapeutic direction is toward bringing the patient into the world of reality. This means that, while we tolerate and track the patient's regressive trends, we do not ourselves regress.

Intuitive and emphatic interventions and the obliteration of ego boundaries contain the danger that the therapist's unconscious needs are being served. We are also skeptical about whether these serve the patient. Freud's technical concept of "evenly suspended attention" pro-vides for the broadest range of receptivity to the patient's signals. It also provides the safest and most reliable measure of the therapist's own feelings and reactions. There is little doubt, however, that receptivity to the patient's communications has higher priority; the therapist's own inner reflections are to be put to use to comprehend the patient's material or, failing that, to determine what it is that impedes such comprehension. Such impediment may be the result of the complexities of the material, or may be attributable to the therapist's blind spots, calling for self-analysis. While this may frequently be necessary, emphasis properly belongs upon the patient's communications. Especially do we need the patient's confirmation of the results of our own introspection in order to make certain that our conclusions refer to the patient and not to our own unconscious.

Addenda to theory have not simplified our technical task. Although theory is now far more complex than in Freud's time, it is also more effective in the treatment of understructured patients who cannot use the classical method. Because the techniques are not yet as refined as we believe they will become, there is much trial and error. But the fortunate therapist can look forward, in his or her own professional development, to the time when these difficulties are experienced not as failures, but as interesting and rewarding challenges which enable us to enhance our skills, extend our knowledge, and also contribute to an expanded theory of technique.

CHAPTER 16
TERMINATION

FREUD (1937) believed that there is a natural termination to an analysis. It comes about when the patient is no longer suffering; when repressed material has been made conscious; when much that had been unintelligible has been explained; when the resistances have been conquered. With those accomplishments there is assurance that the pathological process will not be repeated.

Nevertheless, Freud was not optimistic about achieving such optimal results in all instances. He remained in awe of the strength of the drives. Not until the end of his life did he have the germ of the idea that we have elaborated upon—that both drives might serve developmental purposes. In 1940 Freud describes anew the functions of the drives. Now he believes that libidinal drive seeks to connect while the aggressive drive seeks to sever connections. Because he retained his belief in the death instinct to the end, the aggressive drive, to Freud, could only destroy in the process of severing connections.

Freud's writings fall into three categories: those that are basic and cannot be altered without doing violence to all of psychoanalytic theory; those that he himself revised and modified; and those that belong more in the philosophical than the theoretical realm. The concept of a death instinct is a philosophical one. Many analysts feel entirely comfortable in discarding Freud's philosophical writings while retaining his theoretical concepts.

We have shown in our discussion of the waning of the Oedipus complex that to regard the severing of connections as destructive is to state that growth destroys. That position is opposite to the one to which we subscribe—that growth is essential for life to go forward and to renew. It is the *failure* to sever connections that is in fact destructive. If birth does not take place at term, mother and child perish. This is as true in psychology as in biology. If the child does not separate and individuate, he or she remains psychologically part of another person, unable to fulfill his or her destiny as an individual.

Our position, then, is that it is destructive when separation fails to take place at the appropriate time. This attitude applies to many stages of treatment, and perhaps especially to termination. Psychoanalytic communications are rife with the word *stalemate*. Can that be because psychoanalytic thought is pervaded by the philosophy of destruction? Freud's influence is, quite naturally, so powerful that even those analysts who have discarded the death instinct tend nevertheless to regard separation as destructive.

We have shown the retarding influence of the persistence of the death instinct upon theories of oedipal resolution. Its effect extends not only to the Oedipus complex, but to all aspects of the treatment process, and perhaps most markedly to the process of termination. In essence it represents a subtle and often unrecognizable opposition to autonomy. An outstanding example of the pernicious influence of this growth-retarding point of view is the tendency to regard resistance in pejorative terms, as oppositional and destructive rather than defensive. Hartmann (personal communication) regarded all defense as initially adaptive— that is, as the best solution at the time; only later in life does it tend to become maladaptive.

The idea of a termination "phase" calls for modification because it implies that termination is not an issue before that so-called phase arrives. We think of termination as a natural eventuality when autonomy has been promoted throughout the treatment. In that sense termination, too, is being promoted continuously. The end of treatment comes about when autonomous functioning has reached its optimal level. We shall have more to say about that after we deal with the literature on termination.

Freud's awe of the strength of the drives led him to believe that they can overpower the ego in some instances, such as in psychosis. Only with the advent of modern ego psychology, with its emphasis upon development, has it become possible to see that connection, disconnection, and reconnection are vital to life. The reason to fear the strength of the drives fades as we understand that the superordinate ego orchestrates the entire psychic apparatus to make the drives fit into the overall purpose of achieving and maintaining equilibrium. The orchestra need not be dominated by the timpani. Our proposal of a superordinate ego—central steering organization—adds emphasis to the concept of organization that we elaborated in 1979. The conductor guides the individual instrumentalists to blend in with his overall purpose.

Although Freud introduced thoughts about termination that have been taken up and elaborated upon by many others, he also had the realistic idea that analysis is, in a certain sense, interminable. One can only deal with the pressures from the id that arise in the course of the analysis, he thought. Here, too, modern ego psychology gives matters a more optimistic cast. If the structure is strengthened, and if the superordinate ego is enabled to function more effectively, there is far less reason to fear the resurgence of drive pressures when life's circumstances threaten to bring them to the fore. That there is always the potential for temporary disequilibrium when demands of the id become too great is, of course, to be acknowledged. But if the organism can then rely upon the superordinate ego to right matters, the problem is less pressing. Where needed, there are therapeutic measures that may be employed to come to the aid of the superordinate ego. This differs radically from the notion that, where the id is too powerful, not only the ego but the analyst, too, is helpless.

Most analysts concur with Freud's conclusion that analysis is interminable. Nevertheless, it was believed for a very long time that neurosis can be cured once and for all. The reasoning was that, since neurosis originates in failure to resolve the oedipal conflict, the pathological compromise, it was thought, is reached in final form in childhood. Hence the phrase "infantile neurosis." Psychic structure, it was believed, is complete before latency.

When child analysis was introduced by Melanie Klein and Anna Freud, despite their enormous differences in theory and practice, analysts were led to believe that the psychoanalysis of children could cure neurosis at its very inception. Indeed, Freud tried to help the father of Little Hans do just that even before child analysis became a speciality. The logical belief followed that individuals analyzed in childhood would not be subject to neurosis in adulthood.

It was not until the Amsterdam Congress of the International Psycho-

Analytical Association in 1965 that that belief was shattered. The analysts attending the congress were familiar with Berta Bornstein's analysis of Frankie (1945) because she had described it in great detail in *The Psychoanalytic Study of the Child.* She treated Frankie in childhood for an "infantile neurosis" and felt confident that she had left no stone unturned in dealing with his conflicts. It came as a surprise to those attending the congress to learn that, in the intervening years, Frankie had had problems as a young adult and that she had had to refer him for another analysis.

As a child, Frankie had been phobic. Bornstein made the classical assumption that this was evidence of anxiety hysteria based in oedipal conflict. Samuel Ritvo, the analyst of Frankie as an adult, reported to the congress in detail about Frankie's reanalysis. According to Ritvo, Frankie as a young adult had an obsessional neurosis. But some of the discussants at the congress questioned whether this was indeed a structured neurosis. True, Bornstein had succeeded in her objective of substituting obsessional mechanisms for Frankie's phobias. At issue is the important diagnostic question whether obsessional symptoms can be present in the understructured as well as in the structured personality. (See chapter 9.)

Several important lessons were learned at that congress—principally that a childhood analysis, no matter how thorough, cannot take a person beyond his or her age-appropriate developmental level. In fact, it does well to accomplish just that. Bornstein had succeeded in relieving Frankie of his childhood phobias, but she had not been able, in advance of adolescence and early adulthood, to deal with that which was yet to come in normal developmental progression. In fact, a question arose in the minds of many analysts—had Bornstein gone too far in her therapeutic zeal in the attempt to forestall future neurosis? In her defense it must be pointed out that she was operating with the accepted theory of her time. But in retrospect it appears that Frankie would have been better served if she had terminated his treatment when she had brought him to his age-appropriate developmental level. In fact, she went far beyond that in the hope of precluding later conflict.

But even more than the important discovery that childhood neurosis cannot be cured once and for all developed out of that congress. Thanks to Bornstein's detailed report, her diagnosis of Frankie—anxiety hysteria—was reconsidered in the light of newer theory that was in the very process of being developed. Greenson, speaking from the floor, thought that there were certain unresolved features in Frankie's difficult relationship with his preoedipal mother which suggested that Frankie had suffered from a borderline, not a neurotic, condition. (That the pathology would today be regarded as prestructural is borne out by Bornstein's account of the "King Boo Boo" episode.)

Also speaking from the floor, Winnicott discussed the problems of early object relations as he saw them in the life history. He commented especially on the fact that Frankie had been strapped in his high chair for hours at a time, from which he concluded that Frankie's first object had been a chair. While one might differ with that, the mere introduction of the concept of early object relations was innovative at that time.

Blos (1962) demonstrated that the oedipal conflict (and the separation-individuation process) undergoes a second round in adolescence. We have already referred to our own addenda to developmental theory, that young adulthood and marriage are developmental phases, and to Benedek's view that parenthood is a developmental phase. A historical survey of developmental theories is not complete unless it mentions also that Erikson (1959) proposed that there are stages of development throughout the life cycle. Although his point of view is more sociological than some theorists, particularly Jacobson, welcome, it is nevertheless a developmental point of view.

The issue of termination thus far in our discussion is qualified by the interrelated considerations that analysis can only deal with the material that comes to light at that time, as Freud suggested; and analysis can only bring a person to the age-appropriate developmental level, as was learned from the reanalysis of Frankie. Further elaboration of the problem of termination by developmental theory takes us into the realm of object relations. Termination, after all, involves separation, which the ego psychologists, especially Mahler, have so brilliantly illuminated. It is therefore in place to suggest that the process of separation-individuation cannot be omitted from consideration of the process of termination. Nevertheless, our review of the literature indicates that it has been omitted, not only by the early authors who did not have that theory available, but by some contemporary authors who appear simply to have ignored it.

The earlier writers appear, by and large, also to have overlooked Freud's reservations about termination and his conclusion that, when all is done, analysis has to be regarded as interminable. Overlooked, too, is his suggestion that analysts return for reanalysis every five years. Why analysts and not ordinary mortals? Presumably because the id of the analyst is so bombarded in his or her daily work that a "booster" analysis becomes necessary. This suggestion may be argued pro and con, but the fact is that it is honored in the breach. Analysts do return for reanalysis, probably more often than others, but not in obedience to Freud's suggestion. Rather, they return for personal reasons.

The institutionalization of psychoanalysis makes reanalysis necessary for analysts in many instances. Because analysis is a prime requirement for candidacy in a psychoanalytic institute, candidates are analyzed with the training committee present in fantasy behind the analyst's chair, influencing both analyst and analysand. The objective of being adequately analyzed inevitably clashes, at some point, with the objective of "passing," of meeting the requirements of the training institute. After all, we are brought up under an educational system that uses the completion of requirements as rites of passage. The urgency to *do well* supersedes the analytic requirement to *tell all*. As a result, many candidates, having met the requirements of the institute, undertake reanalysis. Graduates have been known to say, "That was for the institute; this one is for me." Sometimes they refer to the reanalysis as a "retread." Kairys (1964) believes that training analyses are necessarily incomplete, as does Ekstein (1965). Calef and Weinshel (1983) go far beyond that. They contend that all terminations, not only of candidates, are experienced as incomplete because oedipal wishes remain unconsummated.

By no means are we implying that analytic candidates are not to be analyzed. How this can be accomplished as successfully as possible given the handicaps of institutionalized education is beyond our scope here.

There is another implication contained in the issue of reanalysis. The adequacy of the first analysis comes into question. This leads to still another question—can an analysis be valid if future advances in theory construction are not available at the time when a given analysis takes place? The logic of this question reduces to the absurd—that therefore all analyses are to be held in abeyance until the last word is known.

A participant in one of our workshops (1984) raised that question when we had presented some of the theory that we are proposing here. He asked whether we mean to imply that all analyses that were conducted before are invalid. Our answer is "Of course not." Since we were teaching ego psychology and beyond at that workshop, we answered that all talented analysts are ego psychologists even when they do not conceptualize it. We cited the example of Ella Freeman Sharpe (1950), who did not live to see ego psychology evolve very far, but who was an intuitive ego psychologist. All analysts who are as concerned with promotion of autonomy as they are with interpretation of conflict are using ego psychology, whether intuitively or in conceptual form.

Because we have so often been misunderstood on the matter of autonomy, we find it necessary to reiterate that Hartmann defined ego autonomy as the relative independence of the ego from the drives. This has little or nothing to do with the patient's declarations of independence from the analyst. While the patient, usually in the throes of a negative transference, may declare his or her readiness to terminate treatment, it is the analyst's responsibility to know whether this is an expression of true ego autonomy or whether it represents infantile negativism and hostility. We refer once again to Kris' "Good Hour" paper, in which he makes this important distinction.

Firestein (1978) has competently reviewed the early literature on termination, and so we refer to some of it only for the purpose of adding comments from developmental theory. Not to be omitted here is Freud's criterion of mental health as the ability to love and work. We find this especially cogent because one sees so many patients who have a capacity to work, but are unable to form adequate object relationships. We have described them in terms of the superordinate ego. They can work because they are innately endowed with talent, but they cannot love because object relations remain undeveloped.

Hoffer (1950) stresses making the unconscious conscious because, at that time, it was still believed that repressed memories are neurosogenic. There remains a shade of the toxic theory of anxiety in this view of toxicity as causative, although Freud had long before (1926a) revised that first theory of anxiety. Perhaps because of the medical model of a focus of infection, the belief that some noxious influence is responsible for neurosis tended to persist despite having been superseded by conflict theory. As we have described in our discussion of seeking the truth, making the unconscious conscious remained the goal of psychoanalysis for a very long time. Not until Kris (1956a) showed that the patterning of experience rather than the uncovering of single memories is a more effective pursuit did the emphasis shift away from the search for *the* toxic memory.

Balint (1950), in conformity with the theory of the time, stresses genital primacy as an objective of analysis. By implication, termination is appropriate when that goal has been reached. He approaches an object relations point of view without the means to conceptualize it by referring, as a criterion for termination, to the ability to maintain a genital relationship with the partner during temporary dissatisfactions. That refers, not to sex, but to a level of object relations that involves regard for the object. Hartmann gave his original lecture to the Vienna Psychoanalytic Society in 1937, and was to develop the concept of object constancy as the ability to retain a constant mental representation of the object regardless of the state of need. Maintenance of a genital relationship during temporary dissatisfactions states the same thought. It is likely that Balint was present at that lecture, or was influenced by it from having read it in the original German long before its English translation in 1958.

Rickman (1950), as would any analyst of that time, stresses orgastic capacity. It was not until the *Panel on Genital Primacy* (Ross 1970) that analysts began to look at the clinical fact that understructured patients can be orgastic, while some structured patients, women in particular, are not. The conclusion began to be drawn, from comments from the floor by one of us (GB), that the very disturbed, even psychotic, women can be orgastic by direct discharge because she lacks the far higher level of object relations of her neurotic sister; the neurotic woman is "encumbered" by complex oedipal object relations which stand in the way of sexual pleasure. Kestenberg (1956) had already alluded to this. The capacity for orgasm, by this reasoning, diminishes in importance as a criterion for termination. Rickman also introduces object relations considerations by referring to the capacity to mourn as another criterion for termination.

Nunberg (1954) was one of the first to be dissatisfied with symptom relief as a criterion. He looked for structural criteria, such as whether conflicts had been worked through. Missing, because it was not known at that time, was that structural considerations extend to the technique of promotion of structuralization where structure if deficient.

Glover (1955) took an extensive survey of psychoanalysts of that time to ascertain their criteria for termination. From that data he divided the termination process into two phases. The principal feature of the first phase is "transference weaning." This conveys the flavor of separation, although Glover could not have couched it in such terms. It is related, loosely, to Rickman's thoughts about the capacity to mourn.

Glover also stresses that symptoms tend to become exacerbated in the termination phase. This phenomenon has been observed over and over again by many analysts. The patient resumes his or her symptoms as though to demonstrate that the cure has not yet been completed. We question whether the resumption of symptoms is an inevitable feature of the termination phase. We suspect that it occurs when termination is introduced by the analyst before the patient is ready to sever the transferential object connection—the analyst insists upon termination without having taken the object relations aspects sufficiently into account. The focus, in such instances, is upon symptom relief and the resolution of intersystemic conflict to the exclusion of intrasystemic conflict and of allowing the patient's growing ego autonomy to dictate termination. It occurs to us that the resumption of symptoms is a form of communication to an analyst too intent upon termination while the patient is still unable to separate. The patient has no other means of informing the analyst short of teaching him or her separation-individuation theory. Exacerbation of symptoms, therefore, is a message. The patient acts that which cannot be verbalized.

Another consideration for these times is that analysts are seeing fewer symptom neuroses. This reduces the matter of symptom cure as a criterion for termination. Even where there are symptoms, which might recur later in life, the truth that Nunberg approached—that the structure is more important than the symptomatology—remains compelling. Eissler (1953) elaborated upon this matter.

Glover, too, in describing the second termination phase, stresses structural change over symptom cure. He also adds the important matter of termination dreams as heralds of readiness for termination. Cavenar and Nash (1976) refer to "signal" dreams for termination. There is no doubt that dreams can be important signals of approaching readiness to terminate. Kris' "Good Hour" paper stresses that the *style* in which the dream is used can be a signal; more usual is that the *content* informs of approaching termination.

A dream about arrival at a destination suggests termination. Dreams are usually somewhat more subtle than that: "I was working on a puzzle which I completed by myself." An example of transference dream that communicates that the analyst is missing the termination theme: "We were walking along a path together. You grasped my hand. I felt pleased. But it was difficult for us to walk side by side that way because the path was so narrow."

It came as a considerable surprise to find, in our survey of the literature, that separation-individuation theory is so little used, even in refutation. In most instances it was not even considered. We were also surprised to note that Kris' thoughts about the "Good Hour" as the signal that termination is nigh are overlooked.

When separation-individuation theory was still quite new, one of us (G. Blanck 1966) had an inkling that the early-in-life experiences of separation have some bearing upon the manner in which termination is to be conducted. The thought was that the separations in early life, in particular the traumatic ones, are to be taken into account by the analyst in "tailoring" the termination so as not to repeat and thereby reinforce the growth-retarding aspects of separation.

Advice about "tailoring" includes suggesting what not to do as well as providing guidelines about what to do. One must be acutely attuned to the separation trauma in the patient's early life. When termination approaches, the patient who has been hurt by earlier separations will place subtle temptations before the analyst, unconsciously inviting him or her to repeat the trauma. It is of the utmost importance to be alert to these in order assiduously to avoid them.

A patient who had felt abandoned by his parents in early life because essential surgery necessitated long hospitalization was in fact abandoned in adolescence when the parents divorced. After several years of analysis he told the analyst that he was ready to terminate. The analyst accepted that and ended shortly thereafter. The patient told the second analyst that he had hoped, during that last session, that the first analyst would challenge his readiness to leave, that it was exceedingly painful when he realized that the analyst fell into his trap.

Another patient whose mother had died when she was ten years old was sent to boarding school because her father thought that would be the best solution to providing for her daily care. The patient was, of course, miserably homesick as well as in mourning for her mother. As an adult patient, she taunted the analyst where she sensed that she might engender a negative countertransference, mercilessly criticizing the analyst's appearance, habits, clothing, office decor, and the like. The analyst used the countertransference constructively by interpreting that she was inviting him to dismiss her prematurely.

"Tailoring" often has to be done in the face of these kinds of obstacles erected by the patient's unconscious need to repeat. The patient whose parents have died, or have disappeared for other reasons, should probably not be terminated in the spring if the analyst takes a summer vacation. Time should be arranged for working through the termination while the analyst remains in place.

A patient whose father deserted the family when the patient was eight years old approached a reasonable conclusion of his treatment toward the spring of the fourth year. He knew from previous years that the analyst would probably go on vacation in July, and so he pressed for termination at the end of May. It took repeated interpretation of the repetition to try to keep the patient from deserting the analyst before the analyst would "desert" him. He even accused the analyst of trying to keep him on in order to keep his schedule filled, assuming that the analyst could not begin a new case shortly before leaving on vacation. Thus he wanted to deprive as well as abandon. It was difficult to convince him that it was in his best interest to go through a termination that would be different from his life experience. This meant not only remaining in treatment until the analyst's vacation, but returning for a brief period after the analyst's return. In the patient's conscious arguments this would constitute an unnecessary drain on his finances. In the analyst's mind it would be a worthwhile investment in assuring that later life would not be troubled by traumatic endings.

For persons who reach self and object constancy for the first time through treatment, the physical as well as psychological separation from the analyst is a new experience that requires working through. This calls for a special kind of tailoring, for here one is not dealing with a repetition. This is one of the very few aspects of treatment that involve a real experience. Treatment of the structured patient should never be conducted in the experiential realm.

After a few years of analysis there is more than one clue about a patient's readiness to deal with the analyst's absence. These clues come, most often, around the analyst's vacations. If the patient has suffered severe separation anxiety at the analyst's first vacation, one would expect that the treatment would have dealt with it in the course of the years so that the anxiety would attenuate. If separation continues to be a problem, it probably means that the treatment has not yet resolved separation issues. Clearly, we do not insist upon termination while it is too painful for the patient. This does not mean that mild, normal sadness that accompanies termination is reason to keep the patient in treatment.

But does concern about separation anxiety lead to the danger of overly prolonged treatment? We think not *if* it is clear that the analyst does not need the patient because of his or her own separation anxiety. If the patient is needed, reanalysis is indicated for the analyst. At the very least he or she should examine the countertransference. The conclusion from the literature that we have examined is that it is more likely that the analyst is too eager to dismiss the patient out of therapeutic zeal, need to have a successfully terminated case, fear that one's colleagues will think that a case is taking too long. This should allay the layperson's fear that analysts tend to keep patients too long.

Firestein studied the termination of eight analytic cases at the Treatment Center of the New York Psychoanalytic Institute. In all instances anxiety about termination is evident to the analyst, the supervisor, and the investigator. However, it is analyzed as resistance rather than in terms of separation-individuation theory, although Firestein comes tantalizingly close to consideration of separation anxiety when he says: "Not surprisingly, the prospect of termination evokes memories of similar experiences of disappointment and/or turning away, especially with parents, at an earlier period of life" (1978:204–205).

Here the well-known concept of repetition in the transference is used. In contrast with the specificity of Mahler's work, that appears global. We are left to wonder whether the reference is to rapprochement disappointment, or to disappointment at some other developmental phase. Also overlooked is that some early, preverbal experiences are not interpretable. But in either event, repetition can only cease where the precise trauma being repeated is identified and worked through. Our impression of some of the terminations that Firestein has studied is that there was disappointment in reality; the analyst pushed termination while the patient was not yet ready.

The developmental point of view appears decisively in the literature with a paper by E. Ticho (1972). He defines mental illness as an interruption or distortion of normal developmental processes. Termination, he believes, becomes appropriate when development is resumed. The first move for termination should come from the patient, he advocates, but the decision to terminate should be jointly agreed upon. We would agree that a joint decision is desirable in all cases, and we would add that it is particularly pertinent in those instances in which self and object relations were at odds in early life. Ticho also stresses the nature of the countertransference in this context. It exists, he says, truly in counterpart to the transference. It can thereby precipitate too abrupt a termination of an analysis, or it can prolong it.

Some of the implications of the developmental position require further discussion. In stating that the very goal of treatment is the resumption of development (which of course includes the attainment of autonomy), one provides a guideline for termination not only in the psychoanalysis of neurosis, but in psychotherapy of the understructured patient. If one limits the goal to resolution of the oedipal conflict, the objective is narrowed even in the psychoanalysis of the structured patient. To regard the Oedipus complex as the fourth organizer of the psyche, on the other hand, is consistent with a developmental slant that does not limit the treatment to that one facet of the totality of development. The Oedipus complex is important. The three preceding organizers of the psyche are equally important. They play different roles in normal development and in the etiology of pathology. We have already described how preoedipal organization influences the nature and quality of the Oedipus complex.

Analysis has been sharply distinguished from psychotherapy of the understructured patient because the oedipal conflict has been seen as something different from the developmental problems of the understructured patient. But if we regard the Oedipus complex as a fourth organizer, it differs from earlier levels of organization only in its complexity, not in its fundamental nature. It represents a more complex level of object relations. As part of a continuum of psychological development, however, its similarity to the organizers that precede it overrides the particularity of its difference.

It is most often not possible to bring the understructured patient to resolution of the oedipal conflict. Although that remains a goal in the treatment of neurosis, only sometimes is this a realistic goal for the understructured patient. Probably the preponderance of understructured patients can be content with the attainment of self and object constancy, with increased competence in the functioning of the superordinate ego, and do not have the time, ambition, talent, persistence, patience, and financial resources necessary to undertake the extensive treatment involved in moving beyond satisfactory functioning into areas of intersystemic conflict. We described the case of Mr. Baker in 1974 as one in which analysis of the conflictual elements was undertaken. But we noted that, at attainment of self and object constancy, the patient has the right to choose whether to go on to analysis then and there, to postpone it to a later time, or to live productively and contentedly with the therapeutic gains that have been made. The former borderline or narcissistic patient who attains self and object constancy experiences the accompanying attainment of identity with such pleasure that he or she is likely to wish to try this out in real life. Sometimes such patients return at a later time to deal with conflictual matters.

The developmental position, however, does not permeate the literature. Two papers that appeared after Ticho's overlook the developmental point of view.

Shane and Shane (1984) review the traditional thinking about termination—that it is a distinct phase in the analytic process, that a mutually agreed upon date is set, that there is likely to be a recurrence of symptoms during the termination phase. They agree with the traditional view that structural change is the goal of analysis and therefore that such change must take place if the analysis is to be terminated successfully. However, they introduce a paradox—that the transference neurosis is immutable. We are left to wonder how the neurosis can be cured by the long-accepted criterion of alteration in the structure while the transference neurosis remains unaltered. In chapter 8 we described the process whereby transference potential is created, and we suggested that transference involves compromised reality testing. If Shane and Shane mean that even with successful analysis only a vision of reality rather than true reality remains, we can agree with them. However, that refers to transference. Transference neurosis includes the neurotic structure that the very design of analysis seeks to alter. We would conclude, therefore, that the transference neurosis would alter as the neurosis alters, but that transference per se is never completely eliminated.

Goldberg and Marcus (1985) contrast a "natural" termination with the traditional process. They describe a case in which it seemed appropriate to end without having set a date for termination and without completing a distinct termination phase. This, they contend, is more natural than the formal termination process. Overlooked is the theoretical richness of Kris' description of termination as involving the acquisition of ego autonomy. That description of the patient's readiness for termination seems more truly "natural." Our own addendum to Kris' contribution involves the transfer of the functions of the analyst so that the patient can go on alone.

The process of termination, in our view, begins with the first consultation or even before—in the telephone call that arranges for the first consultation. At that stage termination is farthest from the patient's mind, nor need it be uppermost in the mind of the therapist. There is other work to be done—resistances to be understood, structuralization to be evaluated, level of object relations to be considered, and the other criteria on the Fulcrum of Development to be sought out where possible to complete the diagnostic picture. Decisions need to be made about the form of treatment and frequency of sessions.

Yet the promotion of autonomy as a goal exerts its influence throughout the contact between a person in need of treatment and a person who professes to be competent to treat. The attitude that guides us is that, in the end, the patient will be more autonomous than at the beginning. This cannot be a matter of chronology; it is all-pervasive. It is in that sense that we say, albeit somewhat dramatically, that termination is somewhere in the background even at the time of arranging for the first consultation.

Psychoanalytic developmental psychology does not imply that treatment consists of reparenting. We object to the simplistic view that the therapist represents the parent, having explained that pathology is far too complex to respond to an attempt to bring up the patient all over again. But there remains a sense in which the therapist is *in loco parentis*. With regard to incestuous wishes, for example, patient and analyst may both be free in reality to carry on a love affair, but that is not the purpose for which they are together. Regardless of whether there is much difference in their ages, for analytic purposes the analyst always represents a parental, and often an oedipal, figure.

Similarly, with regard to those functions of the object representations that the patient is not yet able to take over, the therapist is a temporary guardian. But such guardianship involves constant alertness to opportunities to promote the transfer of functions of the representation of the analyst to the self representation. Among the analyst's functions is that of bringing the treatment to a comfortable end some day. One way of defining termination is that it comes about when the functions of the analyst are no longer needed because the terminating patient knows how to carry on alone. This does not mean that the ex-patient actively performs daily self-analysis. Now and then the former patient analyzes a dream, some anxiety, an act that is puzzling or questionable. The process as well as the function retains a momentum that is never lost. We are thus led full circle to Freud's position that analysis is, after all, interminable. Only the joint venture terminates.

The point in the treatment process at which the person becomes capable of taking over varies from one individual to another because it is a factor of the combination of innate endowment, life experience, and the functioning of the superordinate ego. We refer here to that unique and individual creation—the form of object relations that is the resultant of self and object experiences. The treatment, whether psychotherapy or psychoanalysis, brings the patient to the level where the object representation is separate from the self representation, at least. At most, the therapist or analyst has been used as the catalyst of development toward the consolidation of each of the four organizers of the psyche where that had not been accomplished before.

The philosophy that we are advocating requires that the interventions be phrased, even early in treatment, with an eye and ear toward making the ending as smooth as possible. Each intervention is to be regarded as a small step toward the end goal; interventions are to be couched in terms that address both the immediate purpose and the ultimate one. In the beginning the immediate purpose dominates; toward the middle the balance shifts more toward preparing for the end. This means that guardianship of autonomy is a continuous process and, of overriding importance, that termination does not begin in the termination phase but is a process of "letting go" in appropriate dosages throughout treatment.

A patient, upon ending a session in the first quarter of treatment, asked to use the telephone. The analyst said that there was a public phone in the lobby of the building. This became a theme during the remainder of the treatment, sometimes in an apparently negative way when the patient complained bitterly about the analyst's callousness, sometimes more positive sounding as the patient began to appreciate that he was being encouraged by the very "callousness" to do for himself that which was possible for him to do. Every experienced analyst will recognize that even the negatively tinged complaints were growth promoting. It seems almost superfluous to say that the analyst did not defend himself against such "criticism" but rode out the storm with complete confidence that he had acted correctly.

The patient appreciated, ultimately, that this was different from his mother's overdoing. She had not turned tasks over to him as he grew. As an example, she took him to school long after he was able to go alone, and she made his bed for him until he left for college.

By the termination phase, the fact that he could do many things for himself that had formerly appeared impossible had already been established. Although separation anxiety inevitably arose, termination was far less traumatic than it might have been had not the analysis helped the patient become increasingly autonomous throughout the course of treatment.

Sometimes we take measures that appear to be the opposite of the thrust toward autonomy that we are describing. Patients who are fearful of closeness and dependency, or who are narcissistically distant, must first be encouraged to enter the transference because they do not do so spontaneously as do patients with higher levels of object relations. Encouragement is made by interpretation of the defense, not by persuasion. Yet, during the time that we attempt to engage the patient in a transference or transference-like arrangement, the direction appears to be the opposite of setting the patient free. Every knowledgeable therapist and analyst knows, however, that in order to be helped out of it, the patient must first be helped into it. Even when we have to go in that direction, therefore, we know that it is for the purpose of enabling the patient to terminate, ultimately, with a greater degree of autonomy than at the beginning of treatment.

Many authors on termination refer to the ability to mourn as a criterion. Certainly, where there has been long and fruitful work together, termination involves sadness for both parties to the therapeutic endeavor. On the countertransference side, we are reminded of Greenacre's (1959) observation that when two people work together, there is a "warming." Patients always wonder, and sometimes ask, whether we like them. Aside from considerations of overgratification, this is a difficult question to answer because an analyst with adequate object relations has a firmer representation of his or her patient toward the end than at the beginning. Because we are privileged to help the patient through this most intimate of treatments, the warming is inevitable and we do feel sad when the patient terminates. We do not regard this as true mourning.

On the patient's side, the analyst becomes more of a real object toward the end of treatment as the transference dissolves. Real objects do not have to be mourned in order to be decathected in the same way as deceased objects. Deceased parents or spouses have to be mourned so that life can be resumed without them. Even in those instances, the object representations do not die; they simply lose cathexis that may then be transferred to new objects in reality. In *The Rose Tattoo* Tennessee Williams depicts a woman whose husband has been killed in an accident. She takes up with a stranger whom she describes as having the body of her husband and the face of a clown. She has not decathected the husband and therefore cannot form a new object connection.

That the analyst has been careful throughout the treatment not to have become a part of the patient's real life is most telling at the time of termination. He or she can be remembered (i.e., the object representation can be retained) after termination without altering life in the outside world. During the course of the analysis or psychotherapy the patient's functioning, including object connections in the real world, has been improved. In the transference the analyst has represented objects from the past more than his or her real self. The process of transference resolution, therefore, involves decathexis of *past* objects more than of the analyst as a real person. It does not seem to us that, as functions are transferred and as the patient becomes more autonomous and thereby less dependent upon past objects, the objects are to be mourned if they are still living. We think of the process of termination as analogous to that which we have already described in the waning of the Oedipus complex. The representation of the object is not lost. But just as oedipal resolution facilitates the transfer of cathexis to objects of one's own generation, resolution of the transference involves the increased capacity to engage in real object relationships.

The analyst or therapist does become more real to the patient toward the end of treatment. That object representation, no longer a transfer figure, is positively cathected because the analyst has been helpful. The function of the kind, understanding, growth-promoting object representation is internalized. Where true self and object constancy obtain, two individuals need not remain in continuous contact for the representations to remain "alive." By the gradual transfer of function, there comes a time in the joint venture when the analyst's contribution becomes superfluous to the operation. The analysis does not terminate;

only the contact with the analyst terminates. It is in that sense that analysis is interminable. The patient can now take over and continue without the actual physical presence of the analyst. The need, not the object representation, wanes.

References

Abelin, E. L. 1971. The role of the father in the separation-individuation process. In John B. McDevitt and Calvin F. Settlage, eds., *Separation-Individuation*, pp. 229–252. New York: International Universities Press.

Arlow, J. A. and C. Brenner. 1964. *Psychoanalytic Concepts and the Structural Theory*. New York: International Universities Press.

Balint. M. 1950. On the termination of analysis. *International Journal of Psycho-Analysis* 31:196–199.

Benedek, T. 1959. Parenthood as a developmental phase. *Journal of the American Psychoanalytic Association* 7:389–417.

Blanck, G. 1966. Some technical implications of ego psychology. *International Journal of Psycho-Analysis* 47:6–13.

Blanck, G. and R. Blanck. 1972. Toward a psychoanalytic developmental psychology. *Journal of the American Psychoanalytic Association* 20:668–710.

—— 1974. *Ego Psychology: Theory and Practice*. New York: Columbia University Press.

—— 1979. *Ego Psychology II: Psychoanalytic Developmental Psychology*. New York: Columbia University Press.

Blanck, R. 1965. The case for individual treatment. *Social Casework*, Family Service Association of America, 46:70–74.

—— 1967. Marriage as a phase of personality development. *Social Casework*, Family Service Association of America, 48:154–160.

—— 1981. The functions of the object representations. Paper given at a symposium of the Department of Psychiatry, Beth Israel Medical Center.

Blanck, R. and G. Blanck. 1968. *Marriage and Personal Development*. New York: Columbia University Press.

———— 1977. The transference object and the real object. *International Journal of Psycho-Analysis* 58:33–44.

Blos, P. 1962. *On Adolescence: A Psychoanalytic Interpretation.* New York: Free Press.

Bornstein, B. 1945. Clinical notes on child analysis. In Ruth Eissler et al., eds., *The Psychoanalytic Study of the Child,* 1:151–166. New York: International Universities Press.

Brazelton, T. B. et al. 1975. Early mother infant reciprocity. *CIBA Symposium.* Amsterdam.

Brazelton, T. B. and J. S. Robey. 1965. Observations of neonatal behavior. *Journal of the American Academy of Child Psychiatry* 4:613.

Brunswick, R. M. 1940. The preoedipal phase of the libido development. *Psychoanalytic Quarterly* 9:293–319.

Calef, V. and E. M. Weinshel. 1983. A note on consummation and termination. *Journal of the American Psychoanalytic Association* 31:619–642.

Cavenar, J. O. and J. L. Nash. 1976. The dream as a signal for termination. *Journal of the American Psychoanalytic Association* 24:425–435.

DSM-III. 1980. *Diagnostic and Statistical Manual of Mental Disorders.* 3d ed. Washington, D.C.: American Psychiatric Association.

Edgcumbe, R. M. 1984. Modes of communication: The differentiation of somatic and verbal expression. In Albert Solnit and Ruth Eissler, eds., *The Psychoanalytic Study of the Child,* 39:137–154. New Haven: Yale University Press.

Edgcumbe, R. and M. Burgner. 1975. The phallic-narcissistic phase: A differentiation between preoedipal and oedipal aspects of phallic development. In Ruth Eissler et al., eds., *The Psychoanalytic Study of the Child* 30:161–180. New Haven: Yale University Press.

Eissler, K. R. 1953. The effect of the structure of the ego on psychoanalytic technique. *Journal of the American Psychoanalytic Association* 1:104–143.

Ekstein, R. 1965. Working through and termination of analysis. *Journal of the American Psychoanalytic Association* 13:57–78.

Erikson, E. H. 1959. Identity and the life cycle. *Psychological Issues.* Monograph 1. New York: International Universities Press.

Fenichel, O. 1941. *Problems of Psychoanalytic Technique.* New York: Psy-choanalytic Quarterly.

—— 1945. *The Psychoanalytic Theory of Neurosis.* New York: Norton.

Firestein, S. K. 1978. *Termination in Psychoanalysis.* New York: Inter-national Universities Press.

Fleming, J. Personal communication.

Freud, A. 1936. *The Ego and the Mechanisms of Defense.* In *The Writings of Anna Freud,* vol. 2. New York: International Universities Press, 1966.

—— 1946. *The Psycho-Analytical Treatment of Children.* London: Imago.

—— 1963. The concept of developmental lines. In Ruth Eissler et al., eds., *The Psychoanalytic Study of the Child,* 18:245–265. New York: International Universities Press.

—— 1965. *Normality and Pathology in Children.* New York: Interna-tional Universities Press.

—— 1966. Obsessional neurosis: A summary of psychoanalytic views. *International Journal of Psycho-Analysis* 47:116–122.

—— 1972. Comments on aggression. *International Journal of Psycho-Analysis* 53:163–172.

Freud, A., H. Nagera and W. E. Freud. 1965. Metapsychological assessment of the adult personality: The adult profile. In Ruth Eissler et al., eds., *The Psychoanalytic Study of the Child,* 20:9–41. New York: International Universities Press.

Freud, S. *The Standard Edition of the Complete Psychological Works of Sig-mund Freud.* 24 vols. James Strachey, tr. and ed. London: Hogarth Press, 1953–1974.

1895. Studies on Hysteria. *S.E.* 2.

1900. The Interpretation of Dreams. *S.E.* 4, 5.

1905a. Fragment of an Analysis of a Case of Hysteria. *S.E.* 8.

1905b. Three Essays on the Theory of Sexuality. *S.E.* 7.

1906. My Views on the Part Played by Sexuality in the Aetiology of the Neuroses. *S.E.* 7.

1909. Notes Upon a Case of Obsessional Neurosis. *S.E.* 10.

1910. Observations on Wild Analysis. *S.E.* 11.

1912a. The Dynamics of Transference. *S.E.* 12.

1912b. Recommendations to Physicians Practising Psychoanalysis. *S.E.* 12.

1913. On Beginning the Treatment (Further Recommendations on the Technique of Psychoanalysis). *S.E.* 12.

1914a. Remembering, Repeating and Working-Through (Further Recommendations on the Technique of Psychoanalysis). *S.E.* 12.

1914b. On Narcissism. *S.E.* 14.

1914c. Observations on Transference-Love (Further Recommendations on the Technique of Psycho-Analysis). *S.E.* 12.

1915. Instincts and Their Vicissitudes. *S.E.* 14.

1916–17. Resistance and repression. Lecture 19, *Introductory Lectures on Psychoanalysis. S.E.* 16.

1917a. Mourning and Melancholia. *S.E.* 14.

1917b. The libido theory and narcissism. Lecture 26, *Introductory Lectures on Psychoanalysis. S.E.* 16.

1920a. Beyond the Pleasure Principle. *S.E.* 18.

1920b. Preface to the fourth edition of the Three Essays on the Theory of Sexuality. *S.E.* 7:133.

1921. Group Psychology and the Analysis of the Ego. *S.E.* 18.

1923. The Ego and the Id. *S.E.* 19.

1923a. The Infantile Genital Organization. *S.E.* 19.

1924. The Dissolution of the Oedipus Complex. *S.E.* 19.

1924a. *The Collected Papers.* Joan Riviere, tr. London: Hogarth Press.

1925. Negation. *S.E.* 19.

1926a. Inhibitions, Symptoms and Anxiety. *S.E.* 20.

1926b. The Question of Lay Analysis. *S.E.* 20.

1930. Civilization and Its Discontents. *S.E.* 21.

1933a. The dissection of the psychical personality. Lecture 31, *New Introductory Lectures. S.E.* 22.

1933b. Femininity. Lecture 33, *New Introductory Lectures. S.E.* 22.

1937. Analysis Terminable and Interminable. *S.E.* 23.

1940. An Outline of Psycho-Analysis. *S.E.* 23.

Friedman, L. 1984. Pictures of treatment by Gill and Schafer. *Psychoanalytic Quarterly* 53:167–207.

Galenson, E. and H. Roiphe. 1976. Some suggested revisions concerning early female development. *Journal of the American Psycho-analytic Association* 24:29–57.

—— 1980. The preoedipal development of the boy. *Journal of the American Psychoanalytic Association* 28:805–828.

Gill, M. M. 1954. Psychoanalysis and exploratory psychotherapy. *Journal of the American Psychoanalytic Association* 2:771–797.

—— 1984. Psychoanalysis and psychotherapy: A revision. *International Review of Psycho-Analysis* 11:161–180.

Gitelson, M. 1952. Re-evaluation of the role of the Oedipus complex. *International Journal of Psycho-Analysis* 33:351–354.

Glover, E. 1932. A psycho-analytic approach to the classification of mental disorders. In *On the Early Development of Mind.* New York: International Universities Press, 1958.

—— 1943. The concept of dissociation. In *On the Early Development of Mind.* New York: International Universities Press, 1958.

—— 1955. *The Technique of Psychoanalysis.* New York: International Universities Press.

—— 1958. Ego distortions. *International Journal of Psycho-Analysis* 39:260–264.

Goldberg, A. and D. Marcus. 1985. "Natural termination": Some comments on ending analysis without setting a date. *Psychoanalytic Quarterly* 54:46–65.

Greenacre, P. 1954. The role of transference. *Journal of the American Psychoanalytic Association* 2:671–684.

—— 1959. Certain technical problems in the transference relationship. *Journal of the American Psychoanalytic Association* 7:484–502.

—— 1972. Problems of overidealization of the analyst and of analysis: Their manifestations in the transference and countertransference relationship. In Ruth Eissler et al., eds., *The Psychoanalytic Study of the Child,* 20:209–219. New York: International Universities Press.

Greenson, R. R. 1965. The working alliance and the transference neurosis. *Psychoanalytic Quarterly* 34:155–181.

—— 1967. *The Technique and Practice of Psychoanalysis.* New York: Hallmark Press.

Grossman, W. I. and W. A. Stewart. 1976. Penis envy. From childhood wish to developmental metaphor. *Journal of the American Psychoanalytic Association* 24:193–212.

Hartmann, H. 1939. *Ego Psychology and the Problem of Adaptation.* New York: International Universities Press, 1958.

—— 1951. Technical implications of ego psychology. *Psychoanalytic Quarterly* 20:31–43.

—— 1964. *Essays in Ego Psychology.* New York: International Universities Press.

—— Personal communication.

Hartmann, H. and E. Kris. 1945. The genetic approach in psychoanalysis. In Ruth Eissler et al., eds., *The Psychoanalytic Study of the Child,* 1:11–30. New York: International Universities Press.

Hartmann, H., E. Kris, and R. M. Loewenstein. 1946. Comments on the formation of psychic structure. In Ruth Eissler et al., eds., *The Psychoanalytic Study of the Child,* 2:11–38. New York: International Universities Press.

—— 1949. Notes on the theory of aggression. In Ruth Eissler et al., eds., *The Psychoanalytic Study of the Child,* 3/4:9–36. New York: International Universities Press.

Hartmann, H. and R. M. Loewenstein. 1962. Notes on the superego. In Ruth Eissler et al., eds., *The Psychoanalytic Study of the Child,* 17:42–81. New York: International Universities Press.

Hinsie, L. E. 1945. *The Person in the Body.* New York: Norton.

Hoffer, W. 1950. Three psychological criteria for the termination of treatment. *International Journal of Psycho-Analysis* 31:194–195.

Horney, K. 1939. *New Ways in Psychoanalysis.* New York: Norton.

Jacobson, E. 1953. Contribution to the metapsychology of cyclothymic depression. In P. Greenacre, ed., *Affective Disorders,* pp. 49–83. New York: International Universities Press.

—— 1954. The self and the object world: Vicissitudes of their infantile cathexes and their influence on ideational and affective development. In Ruth Eissler et al., eds., *The Psychoanalytic Study of the Child,* 9:75–127. New York: International Universities Press.

—— 1964. *The Self and the Object World.* New York: International Universities Press.

—— 1971. *Depression.* New York: International Universities Press.

Joffe, W. G. and J. Sandler. 1968. Comments on the psychoanalytic psychology of adaptation with special reference to the role of affects and the representational world. *International Journal of Psycho-Analysis* 49:445–454.

Kairys, D. 1964. The training analysis. *Psychoanalytic Quarterly* 33:485–512.

Kernberg, O. 1967. Prognostic considerations regarding borderline personality organization. *Journal of the American Psychoanalytic Association* 19:595–635.

—— 1968. The treatment of patients with borderline personality organization. *International Journal of Psycho-Analysis* 49:600–619.

—— 1976. Technical considerations in the treatment of patients with borderline personality organization. *Journal of the American Psychoanalytic Association* 24:795–829.

—— 1982. Self, ego affects and drives. *Journal of the American Psychoanalytic Association* 30:893–918.

Kestenberg, J. S. 1956. Vicissitudes of female sexuality. *Journal of the American Psychoanalytic Association* 4:453–476.

Klein, M. 1948. *Contributions to Psycho-Analysis: 1921–1945.* London: Hogarth Press.

Knight, R. P. 1954. Borderline states. In R. P. Knight and C. R. Friedman, eds., *Psychiatry and Psychology.* New York: International Universities Press.

Kohut, H. 1971. *The Analysis of the Self.* New York: International Universities Press.

—— 1977. *The Restoration of the Self.* New York: International Universities Press.

Kris, E. 1951. Ego psychology and interpretation in psychoanalytic therapy. *Psychoanalytic Quarterly* 20:15–30.

—— 1952. *Psychoanalytic Explorations in Art.* New York: International Universities Press.

—— 1956a. On some vicissitudes of insight in psychoanalysis. *International Journal of Psycho-Analysis* 37:445–455.

—— 1956b. The personal myth. *Journal of the American Psychoanalytic Association* 4:653–681.

—— 1956c. The recovery of childhood memories in psychoanalysis. In Ruth Eissler et al., eds., *The Psychoanalytic Study of the Child,* 11:54–88. New York: International Universities Press.

Lampl-de Groot, J. 1946. The preoedipal phase in the development of the male child. In Ruth Eissler et al., eds., *The Psychoanalytic Study of the Child,* 2:75–83. New York: International Universities Press.

—— 1952. Re-evaluation of the role of the Oedipus complex. *International Journal of Psycho-Analysis* 63:335–342.

Lebovici, S. 1982. The origins and development of the Oedipus complex. *International Journal of Psycho-Analysis* 63:201–215.

Lichtenberg, J. D. 1975. The development of the sense of self. *Journal of the American Psychoanalytic Association* 23:453–484.

Loewald, H. W. 1960. On the therapeutic action of psychoanalysis. *International Journal of Psycho-Analysis* 41:16–35.

—— 1962. Internalization, separation, mourning, and the superego. *Psychoanalytic Quarterly* 31:483–504.

—— 1971. The transference neurosis: Comments on the concept and the phenomenon. *Journal of the American Psychoanalytic Association* 19:54–66.

—— 1972. Freud's conception of the negative therapeutic reaction with comments on instinct theory. *Journal of the American Psychoanalytic Association* 20:235–245.

—— 1973a. On internalization. *International Journal of Psycho-Analysis* 54:9–18.

—— 1973b. Comments on some instinctual manifestations of superego formation. In *Papers on Psychoanalysis,* pp. 326–341. New Haven: Yale University Press, 1980.

—— 1978. Instinct theory, object relations, and psychic structure formation. *Journal of the American Psychoanalytic Association* 26:493–506.

—— 1979. The waning of the Oedipus complex. *Journal of the American Psychoanalytic Association* 27:751–776.

—— 1980. *Papers on Psychoanalysis.* New Haven: Yale University Press.

Loewenstein, R. M. 1951. The problem of interpretation. *Psychoanalytic Quarterly* 20:1–14.

Mahler, M. S. 1952. On child psychosis and schizophrenia: Autistic and symbiotic infantile psychosis. In Ruth Eissler et al., eds., *The Psychoanalytic Study of the Child,* 7:286–305. New York: International Universities Press.

—— 1968. *On Human Symbiosis and the Vicissitudes of Individuation.* New York: International Universities Press.

—— 1980. Personal communication.

Mahler, M. and P. Elkisch. 1953. Some observations on disturbances of the ego in a case of infantile psychosis. In Ruth Eissler et al., eds., *The Psychoanalytic Study of the Child,* 8:252–261. New York: International Universities Press.

Mahler, M., F. Pine and A. Bergman. 1975. *The Psychological Birth of the Human Infant.* New York: Basic Books.

Meissner, W. W. 1970. Notes on identification. I. Origins in Freud. *Psychoanalytic Quarterly* 39:563–589.

—— 1971. Notes on identification. II. Clarification of related concepts. *Psychoanalytic Quarterly* 40:277–302.

—— 1972. Notes on identification. III. The concept of Identification. *Psychoanalytic Quarterly* 41:224–260.

—— 1973. Identification and learning. *Journal of the American Psychoanalytic Association* 21:788–816.

—— 1974. Differentiation and integration of learning and identification in the developmental process. In Chicago Institute for Psychoanalysis, *The Annual of Psychoanalysis,* vol. 2. New York: International Universities Press.

—— 1976. A note on internalization as process. *Psychoanalytic Quarterly* 45:374–393.

—— 1979. Internalization and object relations. *Journal of the American Psychoanalytic Association* 27:345–360.

—— 1980. The problem of internalization and structure formation. *International Journal of Psycho-Analysis* 61:237–248.

Menninger, K. 1958. *Theory of Psychoanalytic Technique.* New York: Basic Books.

Milrod, D. 1982. The wished for self image. In Albert Solnit et al., eds., *The Psychoanalytic Study of the Child,* 37:95–120. New Haven: Yale University Press.

Moore, B. E. and B. D. Fine. 1967. *A Glossary of Psychoanalytic Terms and Concepts.* New York: American Psychoanalytic Association.

Mullahy, P. 1970. *Psychoanalysis and Interpersonal Psychology: The Contributions of Harry Stack Sullivan.* New York: Science House.

Murphy, W. F. 1965. *The Tactics of Psychotherapy.* New York: International Universities Press.

Nunberg. H. 1931. The synthetic function of the ego. *International Journal of Psycho-Analysis* 12:123–140.

—— 1954. Evaluation of the results of psychoanalytic treatment. *International Journal of Psycho-Analysis* 35:2–7.

Osofsky, J. D., ed. 1979. *Handbook of Infant Development.* New York: John Wiley.

Rangell, L. 1959. The nature of conversion. *Journal of the American Psychoanalytic Association* 7:632–662.

—— 1972. Aggression, Oedipus and historical perspective. *International Journal of Psycho-Analysis* 53:3–11.

—— 1982. The self in psychoanalytic theory. *Journal of the American Psychoanalytic Association* 30:863–892.

—— 1985. The object in psychoanalytic theory. *Journal of the American Psychoanalytic Association* 33:301–334.

Rapaport, D. 1959. An historical survey of psychoanalysis. Introduction to *Psychological Issues* 1:5–17.

Rapaport, D. and M. M. Gill. 1959. The points of view and assumptions of metapsychology. In *The Collected Papers of David Rapaport,* pp. 795–811. New York: Basic Books.

Reich, W. 1945. *Character-Analysis: Principles and Technique for Psychoanalysts in Practice and in Training.* New York: Orgone Institute Press.

Rickman, J. 1950. On the criteria for the termination of an analysis. *International Journal of Psycho-Analysis* 31:200–201.

Ritvo, S. 1966. Correlation of a childhood and adult neurosis: Based on the adult neurosis of a reported childhood case. *International Journal of Psycho-Analysis* 47:130–131.

Roiphe, H. and E. Galenson. 1981. *Infantile Origins of Sexual Identity.* New York: International Universities Press.

Ross, J. M. 1982. Oedipus revisited: Laius and the "Laius Complex." In Albert Solnit, et al., eds., *The Psychoanalytic Study of the Child,* 37:169–200. New Haven: Yale University Press.

Ross, N. 1970. The primacy of genitality in the light of ego psychology: Introductory remarks. *Journal of the American Psychoanalytic Association* 17:267–284.

Sander, L. (rep.). 1980. New knowledge about the infant from current research: Implications for psychoanalysis. *Journal of the American Psychoanalytic Association* 28:181–198.

Sandler, J. 1960. The background of safety. *International Journal of Psycho-Analysis* 41:352–356.

Sandler, J. and W. G. Joffe. 1969. Towards a basic psychoanalytic model. *International Journal of Psycho-Analysis* 50:79–90.

Sandler, J. and B. Rosenblatt. 1952. The concept of a representational world. In Ruth Eissler et al., eds., *The Psychoanalytic Study of the Child*, 17:128–145. New York: International Universities Press.

Schafer, R. 1960. The loving and beloved superego in Freud's structural theory. In Ruth Eissler et al., eds., *The Psychoanalytic Study of the Child*, 15:163–190. New York: International Universities Press.

—— 1968. *Aspects of Internalization*. New York: International Universities Press.

—— 1970. The psychoanalytic vision of reality. *International Journal of Psycho-Analysis* 51:279–297.

Shane, M. and E. Shane. 1984. The end phase of analysis: Indicators, functions, and tasks of termination. *Journal of the American Psychoanalytic Association* 32:739–772.

Sharpe, E. F. 1950. *Collected Papers on Psycho-Analysis*. London: Hogarth Press.

Spitz, R. A. 1945. Hospitalism: An inquiry into the genesis of psychiatric conditions in early childhood. In Ruth Eissler et al., eds., *The Psychoanalytic Study of the Child*, 1:52–74. New York: International Universities Press.

—— 1946. Hospitalism: A follow up report. In Ruth Eissler et al., eds., *The Psychoanalytic Study of the Child*, 2:113–117.

—— 1957. *No and Yes*. New York: International Universities Press.

—— 1959. *A Genetic Field Theory of Ego Formation*. New York: International Universities Press.

—— 1965. *The First Year of Life*. New York: International Universities Press.

Stern, D. N. 1976. A microanalysis of mother-infant interaction: Behavior regulating social contact between a mother and her 3 month old twins. In E. Rexford, L. Sander, and T. Shapiro, eds., *Infant Psychiatry*, pp. 113–126. New Haven: Yale University Press.

—— 1980. Panelist. See Sander 1980.

Tarachow, S. 1963. *An Introduction to Psychotherapy.* New York: International Universities Press.

Ticho, E. 1972. Termination of psychoanalysis: Treatment goals, life goals. *Psychoanalytic Quarterly* 41:315–333.

—— 1982. The alternate schools and the self. *Journal of the American Psychoanalytic Association* 30:849–862.

Van der Sterren, H. A. 1952. The "King Oedipus" of Sophocles. *International Journal of Psycho-Analysis* 33:343–350.

Wangh, M. 1959. Structural determinants of phobia. *Journal of the American Psychoanalytic Association* 7:675–695.

Weiss, E. 1960. *The Structure and Dynamics of the Human Mind.* New York: Grune & Stratton.

Zetzel, E. 1956. Current concepts of transference. *International Journal of Psycho-Analysis* 37:369–375.

Name Index

Subject Index

Adaptation, 5, 6, 14, 26, 33, 34, 43, 44, 51, 63, 88, 98, 107, 137
Aggressive drive, 3, 7, 15, 17, 18, 52, 53, 54, 113, 119, 120, 134
Ambitendency, 95, 96
Anxiety, ix, 2, 18, 104, 105, 117
Arrest, 88
Autism, 13, 42, 55, 56
Automatisms, 33
Autonomy, 67, 112, 113, 115, 120, 134, 178, 183, 191–4
Average Expectable Environment, 5

Benign climate, 136, 145–8, 168
Borderline, xi, 4, 13, 122, 130, 138, 154, 181

Castration, 9, 26, 99, 102–4
Change in function, 6, 63, 107, 115
Coenesthetic reception, 12, 33, 46, 47, 50, 56, 140, 147, 157
Conflict, 6, 65, 93–109, 110, 117, 145, 155, 172, 173
Conflict free sphere, 5, 6, 17, 21, 51
Countertransference, 75, 76, 188
Critical periods, xii, 12, 67, 110, 111, 116, 118, 138

Death instinct, 18, 178
Depression, 10, 16, 63, 108, 123
Diagnosis, 108, 122–35, 138

Ego: as battleground, 105, 106; defined, 2, 44, 95; as mediator, 106; as organizer, 10–12, 16, 20, 21, 31, 32, 51, 55, 88, 98, 104, 114, 137, 139, 152, 157, 162, 163; rational, 171, 172; superordinate, 30–36, 43, 44, 46, 48, 49, 58, 61, 79, 81, 82, 95, 98, 102, 105, 107, 108, 111, 134, 136, 139, 140, 153, 157, 178, 179; unconscious, 2, 140; as a whole, 30–33, 44, 61, 140, 153
Ego ideal: defined, 26, 62, 69, 70
Ego psychology, ix, x, xi, 1, 2, 16
Empathy, 14, 146, 175

Fantasy, ix, 46, 74, 152, 171
Female sexuality, xi, 9, 103, 114
Female superego, 9, 10, 101
Fitting together, xii, 5, 36
Free association, 159, 160, 163, 164
Fulcrum of development, 18, 72, 85, 88, 122, 128, 129, 169, 192

Genital primacy, 100, 101, 184
Good hour (Kris), 3, 4, 67, 183, 186

Identification, 6, 8, 20–24, 52, 60, 66, 68–70, 97, 136, 137; selective, 7, 8, 25, 68, 121
Identity, 8, 65, 86, 87, 112; gender, 8, 103
Impotence, 129–32
Internalization, 22, 53, 60–62, 65, 69, 72, 73, 121
Interpretation, xii, 27, 144, 148, 151–58
Introjection, 22, 60

Libido, 7, 18, 53; libidinal object proper, 11, 42